Jacobsens

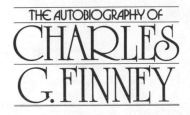

THE AUTOBIOGRAPHY OF
CHARLES G. FINNEY

THE AUTOBIOGRAPHY OF

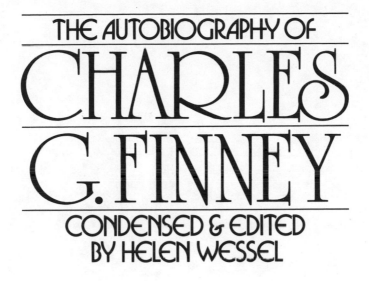

CHARLES G. FINNEY

CONDENSED & EDITED BY HELEN WESSEL

Bethany Fellowship INC.

MINNEAPOLIS, MINNESOTA 55438

Published by Bethany Fellowship, Inc.
6820 Auto Club Road, Minneapolis, Minnesota 55438

Printed in the United States of America

Library of Congress Cataloging in Publication Data:

Finney, Charles Grandison, 1792-1875.
   The autobiography of Charles G. Finney.

   Condensed version of Memoirs of Rev. Charles G. Finney,
originally published in 1876.
    1. Finney, Charles Grandison, 1792-1875.
2. Congregational churches—Clergy—Biography.
3. Clergy—United   States—Biography.   4. Evangelists—
United States—Biography. I. Wessel, Helen Strain, 1924-
II. Title.
BX7260.F47A352 1977   285'.8'0924 [B]   77-2813
ISBN 0-87123-010-0

1

It has pleased God in some measure to connect my name and labors with an extensive movement of the church of Christ, regarded by some as a new era in its progress, especially in relation to revivals. I am only one of many ministers and other servants of Christ who have shared in promoting these revivals, but I have been urged for a number of years by friends to write a history of those revivals with which my name and labors have been connected. My mind seems instinctively to recoil from saying so much of myself as I shall be obliged to do, if I speak honestly of those revivals and of my relation to them. For this reason I have declined up to this time to undertake such a work.

But I have been so often reminded of them and have so often referred to them in all the years of my ministry that I cannot but have strong confidence that I remember them substantially as they occurred. I trust that the church will believe that my statements are in entire accordance with my present memory of those facts. I am now (1867-68) seventy-five years old. Of course I remember things that transpired many years ago more definitely than those of recent occurrence.

I was born in Warren, Litchfield County, Connecticut, August 29, 1792. When I was about two years old my father moved to Oneida County, New York, which was at that time mainly a wilderness. No religious privileges were enjoyed by the people. Very few religious books were to be had. The new settlers, being mostly from New England, almost immediately established common schools, but they had among them very little intelligent preaching of the Gospel.

Neither of my parents were professing Christians, and among our neighbors there were very few religious people. I seldom heard a sermon, unless it was an occasional one from some travelling minister, or some miserable holding forth of an ignorant preacher who would sometimes be found in that country. I remember very well that the ignorance of the preachers whom I heard was such that the people would return from a meeting and spend a considerable time in irrepressible laughter at the strange mistakes which had been made and the absurdities which had been advanced.

In the neighborhood of my father's residence we had just erected a meeting house and settled a minister when my father was induced to move again into the wilderness skirting the southern shore of Lake Ontario, a little south of Sackett's Harbor. Here again I lived for several years, enjoying no better religious privileges than I had in Oneida County.

When about twenty years old I returned to Connecticut, and from there went to New Jersey, near New York City, and engaged in teaching. I taught and studied as best I could, and twice returned to New England and attended high school for a season. While attending high school I thought about going to Yale College. My teacher was a graduate of Yale, but he advised me not to go. He said it would be a loss of time, as I could easily accomplish the whole curriculum of study pursued at that institution in two years whereas it would cost me four years to graduate. He presented such considerations as prevailed with me, and as it resulted, I failed to pursue my school education any further at that time. Later I acquired some knowledge of Latin, Greek, and Hebrew, but I was never a classical scholar, and never possessed so much knowledge of the ancient languages as to think myself capable of independently criticizing our English translation of the Bible.

My parents prevailed on me to go home with them to Jefferson County, New York. After making them a visit I decided to enter, as a student, the law office of Squire W—— at Adams, in that county. This was in 1818.

Up to this time I had never enjoyed what might be called religious privileges. I had never lived in a praying community, except during the periods when I was attending high school in New England, and the religion in that place was of a type not at all calculated to arrest my attention. The preaching was by an aged clergyman, an excellent man and greatly beloved and venerated by his people, but he read his sermons in a manner that left no impression whatever on my mind. He had a monotonous, humdrum way of reading what he had probably written many years before.

To give some idea of his preaching, let me say that his manuscript sermons were just large enough to put into a small Bible. I sat in the balcony and observed that he placed his manuscript in the middle of his Bible, and inserted his fingers at the places of Scripture to be quoted in the reading of his sermon. This made it necessary to hold his Bible in both hands and rendered all gestures with his hands impossible. As he proceeded he would read the passages of Scripture where his fingers were inserted, and thus liberate one finger after another until the fingers of both hands were read out of their places. When his fingers were all read out he was near the close of the sermon.

When he left the meeting I often heard the people speak well of his sermons, and sometimes they would wonder whether he had intended any allusion, in what he said, to what was occurring among them. It seemed to be always a matter of curiosity to know what he was aiming at, especially if there was anything more in his sermon than a dry discussion of doctrine. And this was really quite as good preaching as I had ever listened to in any place. But anyone can judge whether such preaching was calculated to instruct or interest a young man who neither knew nor cared anything about religion.

Thus when I went to Adams to study law, I was almost as ignorant of religion as a heathen. I had been brought up mostly in the woods. I had very little regard for the Lord's Day, and had no definite knowledge of religious truths.

At Adams, for the first time, I sat for a length of time under an educated ministry. Rev. George W. Gale, from Princeton, New Jersey, became pastor of the Presbyterian church in that place soon after I went there. His preaching was of the old school type, that is, it was thoroughly Calvinistic. Whenever he expounded the doctrines, which he seldom did, he would preach what has been called hyper-calvinism. He seemed to take it for granted that his hearers were theologians; therefore he might assume they knew all the great and fundamental doctrines of the Gospel. But I must say I was more perplexed than edified by his preaching.

Up until this time I had never lived where I could attend a regular prayer meeting. Since one was held by the church near our office every week, I used to attend and listen to the prayers, as often as I could be excused from business at that hour.

In studying elementary law, I found the old authors frequently quoting the Scriptures and referring especially to the Mosaic Law as authority for many of the great principles of common law. This excited my curiosity so much that I purchased a Bible, the first I had ever owned. Whenever I found a reference to the Bible made by the law authors, I turned to the passage and consulted it in its connection. This soon led to a new interest in the Bible, and I read and meditated on it much more than I had ever done before. However, much of it I did not understand.

Mr. Gale was in the habit of dropping in at our office frequently and seemed anxious to know what impression his sermons had made on my mind. I used to converse with him freely, and I now think that I sometimes criticized his sermons unmercifully. I raised such objections against his positions as forced themselves upon my attention.

In conversing with him and asking him questions I perceived that his own mind was somewhat confused and that he did not accurately define what he meant by many of the important terms he used. I found it impossible to attach any meaning to many of the terms which he used frequently and with great formality. What did he mean by repentance? Was it a mere feeling of sorrow for sin? Was it altogether a passive state of mind, or did it involve a voluntary element? If it was a change of mind, in what respect was it a change of mind? What did he mean by the term regeneration? What did such language mean when applied to a spiritual change? What did he mean by faith? Was it merely an intellectual state? Was it merely a conviction, or persuasion, that the things stated in the Gospel were true? What did he mean by sanctification? Did it involve any physical change in the subject, or any physical influence on the part of God? I could not tell, nor did he seem to know himself in what sense he used these and similar terms.

We had a great many interesting conversations, but they seemed to stimulate my own mind to inquiry rather than to satisfy me in respect to the truth.

But as I read my Bible and attended the prayer meetings, heard Mr. Gale preach, conversed with him, with the elders of the church, and with others from time to time, I became very restless, A little consideration convinced me that I was by no means in a state of mind to go to heaven if I should die. It seemed to me that there must be something in religion that was of infinite importance, and it was soon settled with me that if the soul was immortal, I needed a great change in my inward state to be prepared for happiness in heaven. But still my mind was not settled as to the truth or falsehood of the Gospel and of the Christian religion. The question, however, was too important to allow me to rest in any uncertainty on the subject.

I was particularly struck with the fact that the prayers that I had listened to from week to week were not, that I could see, answered. Indeed, I understood from their utterances in prayer and from other remarks in their meetings, that those who offered them did not regard them as answered.

When I read my Bible I learned what Christ had said in regard to prayer and answers to prayer. He had said, "Ask, and you shall receive, seek and you shall find, knock and it shall be opened to you. For every one that asks receives, and he that seeks finds, and to him that knocks it shall be opened." I read also what Christ affirms, that God is more willing to give his Holy Spirit to them that ask him than earthly parents are to give good gifts to their children. I heard them pray continually for the outpouring of the Holy Spirit, and as often confess that they did not receive what they asked for.

They exhorted each other to wake up and be active for the Lord and to pray earnestly for a revival, asserting that if they did their duty, prayed for the outpouring of the Spirit, and were in earnest, the Spirit of God would be poured out, they would have a revival, and the impenitent would be converted. But in their prayer and conference meetings they would continually confess that they were making no progress in securing a revival.

This inconsistency—the fact that they prayed so much and were not answered—was a sad stumbling block to me. I knew not what to make of it. I wondered if these persons were not truly Christians, and therefore did not prevail with God, or if I misunderstood the promises and teachings of the Bible on this subject, or if I was to conclude that the Bible was not true. Here was something inexplicable to me, and it seemed at one time that it would almost drive me into skepticism. It seemed to me that the teachings of the Bible did not at all accord with the facts which were before my eyes.

On one occasion when I was in one of the prayer meetings, I was asked if I did not desire that they should pray for me. I told them no, because I did not see that God answered their prayers. I said, "I suppose I need to be prayed for, for I am conscious that I am a sinner, but I do not see that it will do any good for you to pray for me, for you are continually asking, but you do not receive. You have been praying for a revival ever since I have been in Adams, and yet you do not have it. You have been praying for the Holy Spirit to descend upon you, and yet complaining of your leanness. You have prayed enough since I have attended these meetings to have prayed the devil out of Adams if there is any virtue in your prayers. But here you are praying on and complaining still." I was quite in earnest in what I said, and not a little irritable, I think, in consequence of my being brought so continually face to face with religious truth, which was a new state of things to me.

But on further reading of my Bible, it struck me that the reason why their prayers were not answered was because they did not comply with the revealed conditions upon which God had promised to answer prayer. They did not pray in faith, in the sense of expecting God to give them the things that they asked for.

This thought lay for some time in my mind as a confused questioning, rather than in any definite form that could be stated in words. However, this relieved me so far as questions about the truth of the Gospel were concerned, and after struggling in that way for some two or three years, my mind became quite settled that whatever confusion there might be either in my own or in my pastor's mind, or in the mind of the church, the Bible was the true word of God.

This being settled, I was brought face to face with the question whether I would accept Christ as presented in the Gospel, or pursue a worldly course of life. At this period, my mind, as I have since known, was so much impressed by the Holy Spirit that I could not long leave this question unsettled, nor could I long hesitate between the two courses of life presented to me.

2

On a Sunday evening in the autumn of 1821 I made up my mind that I would settle the question of my soul's salvation at once, that if it were possible I would make my peace with God. But as I was very busy in the affairs of the office, I knew that without great firmness of purpose I should never effectively attend to the subject. I therefore resolved to avoid all business and everything that would divert my attention, and to give myself to the work of securing the salvation of my soul. I carried this resolution into execution as sternly and thoroughly as I could. I was, however, obliged to be a good deal in the office. But as the providence of God would have it, I was not much occupied either on Monday or Tuesday, and had opportunity to read my Bible and engage in prayer most of the time.

I was very proud without knowing it. I thought the opinions of others didn't matter, whether they thought this or that in regard to myself. I had in fact been quite faithful in attending prayer meetings and in the degree of attention that I had paid to religion while in Adams. In this respect I had been so faithful as to lead the church at times to think that I must be an anxious inquirer. But I found that when I came to face the question, I was very unwilling to have anyone know I was seeking the salvation of my soul. When I prayed I would only whisper my prayer, after having stuffed the keyhole to the door, lest someone should discover that I was engaged in prayer. Before that time I had my Bible lying on the table with the law books, and it never had occurred to me to be ashamed of being found reading it, anymore than I should be ashamed of being found reading any of my other books.

But after I had addressed myself in earnest to the subject of my own salvation, I kept my Bible, as much as I could, out of sight. If I was reading it when anybody came in, I would throw my law books upon it to create the impression that I had not had it in my hand. Instead of being outspoken and willing to talk with anybody and everybody on the subject as before, I found myself unwilling to converse with anybody. I did not want to see my minister, because I did not want to let him know how I felt. I had no confidence that he would understand my case and give me the direction that I needed. For the same reasons I avoided conversations with the elders of the church or with any of the Christian people. I was ashamed to let them know how I felt on the one hand, and on the other I was afraid they would misdirect me. I felt myself shut up to the Bible.

During Monday and Tuesday my convictions increased, but still it seemed as if my heart grew harder. I could not shed a tear. I could not pray. I had no opportunity to pray above my breath, and frequently I felt that if I could be alone where I could use my voice and let myself out, I should find relief in prayer. I was shy, and avoided, as much as I could, speaking to anybody on the subject. I endeavored to do this in a way that would excite no suspicion in any mind that I was seeking the salvation of my soul.

Tuesday night I had become very nervous, and in the night a strange feeling came over me as if I were about to die. I knew that if I did I would sink down to hell, but I quieted myself as best I could until morning.

At an early hour I started for the office. But just before I arrived at the office, it seemed as if an inward voice confronted me with questions like these: "What are you waiting for? Did you not promise to give your heart to God? And what are you trying to do? Are you endeavoring to work out a righteousness of your own?"

Just at this point the whole question of Gospel salvation opened to my mind in a manner most marvelous. I think I then saw, as clearly as I ever have in my life, the reality and fullness of the atonement of Christ. I saw that his work was a finished work, and that instead of having, or needing, any righteousness of my own to recommend me to God, I had to submit to the righteousness of God through Christ. Gospel salvation seemed to be an offer to be accepted, and that it was full and complete. All that was necessary on my part was my own consent to give up my sins and accept Christ. Salvation was not achieved by my own works, but was to be found entirely in the Lord Jesus Christ, who presented himself before me as my God and my Savior.

Without being distinctly aware of it, I had stopped in the street right where the inward voice seemed to arrest me. How long I remained in that position I cannot say. But after this distinct revelation had stood for some little time before my mind, the question seemed to be, "Will you accept it now, today?"

I replied, "Yes, I will accept it today, or I will die in the attempt."

North of the village and over a hill lay a wooded area in which I walked almost daily when it was pleasant weather. It was now October and the time was past for my frequent walks there. Nevertheless, instead of going to the office I turned and bent my course toward the woods, feeling that I must be alone and away from all human eyes and ears so that I could pour out my prayer to God.

But still my pride wanted to show itself. As I went over the hill it occurred to me that someone might see me and suppose that I was going away to pray. Yet probably there was not a person on earth that would have suspected such a thing had he seen me going. But so great was my pride, and so much was I possessed with the fear of man, that I remember skulking along under the fence until I got so far out of sight that no one from the village could see me. I then penetrated into the woods, about a quarter of a mile, went over on the other side of the hill and found a place where some large trees had fallen across each other, leaving an open place between. There I saw I could make a kind of closet. I crept into this place and knelt down for prayer. As I had turned to go up into the woods I remembered having said, "I will give my heart to God, or I never will come down from there." I remembered repeating this as I went up, "I will give my heart to God before I ever come down again."

But when I attempted to pray I found that my heart would not pray. I had supposed that if I could only be where I could speak aloud without being overheard, I could pray freely. But lo! when I came to try, I was dumb; that is, I had nothing to say to God; or at least I could say but a few words, and those without heart. In attempting to pray I would hear a rustling in the leaves and would stop and look up to see if somebody were not coming. This I did several times.

Finally I found myself fast coming to despair. I said to myself, "I cannot pray. My heart is dead to God, and will not pray." I then reproached myself for having promised to give my heart to God before I left the woods. When I came to try, I found I could not give my heart to God. My inward soul hung back, and there was no going out of my heart to God. I began to feel deeply that it was too late, that I was given up of God and was past hope.

The thought was pressing me of the rashness of my promise that I would give my heart to God that day or die in the attempt. It seemed to me as if that was binding upon my soul, and yet I was going to break my vow. A great sinking and discouragement came over me, and I felt almost too weak to stand upon my knees.

Just at this moment I again thought I heard someone approach me, and I opened my eyes to see whether it were so. But right there the revelation of my pride was distinctly shown to me as the great difficulty that stood in the way. An overwhelming sense of my wickedness in being ashamed to have a human being see me on my knees before God took such powerful possession of me that I cried at the top of my voice and exclaimed that I would not leave that place if all the men on earth and all the devils in hell surrounded me. "What!" I said, "such a degraded sinner as I am, on my knees confessing my sins to the great and holy God, ashamed to have any human being find me on my knees endeavoring to make my peace with my offended God!" The sin appeared awful, infinite. It broke me down before the Lord.

Just at that point this passage of scripture seemed to drop into my mind with a flood of light: "Then shall you go and pray unto me, and I will hearken to you. Then shall you seek me and find me, when you shall search for me with all your heart."

I instantly seized hold of this with my heart. I had intellectually believed the Bible before, but never had the truth been in my mind that faith was a voluntary trust instead of an intellectual state. I was as conscious of trusting at that moment in God's truthfulness as

I was of my own existence. Somehow I knew that that was a passage of scripture, though I do not think I had ever read it. I knew that it was God's word, and God's voice, as it were, that spoke to me.

I cried to him, "Lord, I take Thee at Thy word. Now Thou knowest that I do search for Thee with all my heart, and that I have come here to pray to Thee; and Thou hast promised to hear me."

That seemed to settle the question that I could then, that day, perform my vow. The Spirit seemed to lay stress upon that idea in the text, "When you search for me with all your heart." The question of when, that is of the present time, seemed to fall heavily into my heart. I told the Lord that I would take him at his word, that he could not lie, and that therefore I was sure that he heard my prayer and that he would be found of me.

He then gave me many other promises, both from the Old and the New Testament, especially some most precious promises respecting our Lord Jesus Christ. I never can, in words, make any human being understand how precious and true those promises appeared to me. I took them one after the other as infallible truth, the assertions of God who could not lie. They did not seem so much to fall into my intellect as into my heart, to be put within the grasp of the voluntary powers of my mind, and I seized hold of them with the grasp of a drowning man.

I continued thus to pray and to receive and appropriate promises for a long time. I know not how long. I prayed till my mind became so full that before I was aware of it, I was on my feet and tripping up the ascent toward the road. The question of my being converted had not so much as arisen to my thought, but as I went up, brushing through the leaves and bushes, I remembered saying with great emphasis, "If I am ever converted, I will preach the Gospel."

I soon reached the road that led to the village, and began to reflect upon what had passed. I found that my mind had become most wonderfully quiet and peaceful. I said to myself. "What is this? 1 must have grieved the Holy Spirit entirely away. I have lost all my conviction. I have not a particle of concern about my soul. It must be that the Spirit has left me." "Why!" thought I, "I never was so far from being concerned about my own salvation in my life."

Then I remembered what I had said to God while I was on my knees, that I would take him at his word. Indeed, I remembered a good many things that I had said, and concluded that it was no wonder that the Spirit had left me, that for such a sinner as I to take hold of God's word in that way was presumption, if not blasphemy. I concluded that in my excitement I had grieved the Holy Spirit and perhaps committed the unpardonable sin.

I walked quietly toward the village, and so perfectly quiet was my mind that it seemed as if all nature listened. It was on the 10th of October and a very pleasant day. I had gone into the woods immediately after an early breakfast, and when I returned to the village I found it was lunch time. Yet I had been wholly unconscious of the time that had passed. It appeared to me that I had been gone from the village but a short time.

But how was I to account for the quiet of my mind? I tried to recall my convictions, to get back again the load of sin under which I had been laboring. But all sense of sin, all consciousness of present sin or guilt, had departed from me. I said to myself, "What is this, that I cannot arouse any sense of guilt in my soul, as great a sinner as I am?" I tried in vain to make myself anxious about my present state. I was so quiet and peaceful that I tried to feel concerned about that, lest it should be a result of my having grieved the Spirit away. But take any view of it I would, I could not be anxious at all about my soul and about my spiritual state. The repose of my mind was unspeakably great. I cannot describe it in words. The thought of God was sweet to my mind, and the most profound spiritual tranquillity had taken full possession of me. This was a great mystery, but it did not distress or perplex me.

I went to my lunch but found I had no appetite. I then went to the office and found that Squire W—— had gone to lunch. I took down my bass viol and, as I was accustomed to do, began to play and sing some pieces of sacred music. But as soon as I began to sing those sacred words I began to weep. It seemed as if my heart was all liquid and my feelings were in such a state that I could not hear my own voice in singing without causing my feelings to overflow. I wondered at this and tried to stop my tears, but could not. After trying in vain to stop my tears, I put up my instrument and stopped singing.

After lunch we were engaged in moving our books and furniture to another office. We were very busy and had but little conversation all afternoon. My mind, however, remained in that profoundly tranquil state. There was a great sweetness and tenderness in my thoughts and feelings. Everything appeared to be going right, and nothing seemed to ruffle or disturb me in the least.

Just before evening the thought possessed my mind that as soon as I was alone in the new office, I would try to pray again. I was not going to abandon the subject of religion and give it up at any rate. Therefore, although I no longer had any concern about my soul, still I would continue to pray.

By evening we had the books and furniture adjusted, and I made a good fire in an open fireplace, hoping to spend the evening alone. Just at dark Squire W——, seeing that everything was adjusted, told me good night and went to his home. I had accompanied him to the door, and as I closed the door and turned around my heart seemed to be liquid within me. All my feelings seemed to rise and flow out and the thought of my heart was, "I want to pour my whole soul out to God." The rising of my soul was so great that I rushed into the room back of the front office to pray.

There was no fire and no light in this back room; nevertheless it appeared to me as if it were perfectly light. As I went in and shut the door after me, it seemed as if I met the Lord Jesus Christ face to face. It seemed to me that I saw him as I would see any other man. He said nothing, but looked at me in such a manner as to break me right down at his feet. It seemed to me a reality that he stood before me, and I fell down at his feet and poured out my soul to him. I wept aloud like a child and made such confessions as I could with my choked words. It seemed to me that I bathed his feet with my tears, and yet I had no distinct impression that I touched him.

I must have continued in this state for a good while, but my mind was too much absorbed with the interview to remember anything that I said. As soon as my mind became calm enough I returned to the front office and found that the fire I had made of large wood was nearly burned out. But as I turned and was about to take a seat by the fire, I received a mighty baptism of the Holy Spirit. Without any expectation of it, without ever having the thought in my mind that there was any such thing for me, without any memory of ever hearing the thing mentioned by any person in the world, the Holy Spirit descended upon me in a manner that seemed to go through me, body and soul. I could feel the impression, like a wave of electricity, going through and through me. Indeed it seemed to come in waves of liquid love, for I could not express it in any other way. It seemed like the very breath of

God. I can remember distinctly that it seemed to fan me, like immense wings.

No words can express the wonderful love that was spread abroad in my heart. I wept aloud with joy and love. I literally bellowed out the unspeakable overflow of my heart. These waves came over me, and over me, and over me, one after the other, until I remember crying out, "I shall die if these waves continue to pass over me." I said, "Lord, I cannot bear any more," yet I had no fear of death.

How long I continued in this state, with this baptism continuing to roll over me and go through me, I do not know. But I know it was late in the evening when a member of my choir—for I was the leader of the choir—came into the office to see me. He was a member of the church. He found me in this state of loud weeping, and said to me, "Mr. Finney, what's wrong with you?" I could not answer for some time. He then said, "Are you in pain?"

I gathered myself up as best I could, and replied, "No, but so happy that I cannot live."

He turned and left the office, and in a few minutes returned with one of the elders of the church, whose shop was nearly across the way from our office. This elder was a very serious man and in my presence had been very watchful. I had scarcely ever seen him laugh. When he came in I was very much in the state in which I was when the young man went out to call him. He asked me how I felt and I began to tell him. Instead of saying anything he fell into a most spasmodic laughter. It seemed as if it was impossible for him to keep from laughing from the very bottom of his heart.

There was a young man in the neighborhood, with whom I had been very intimate, who was preparing for college. Our minister, as I afterward learned, had repeatedly talked with him on the subject of religion and warned him against being misled by me. He informed him that I was a very careless young man about religion, and he thought that if he associated much with me, his mind would be diverted and he would not be converted.

After I was converted and this young man was converted, he told me that he had said to Mr. Gale several times, when the latter had warned him about associating so much with me, that my conversations had often affected him more than his preaching. I had, indeed, shared my feelings a good deal with this young man.

But just at the time when I was giving an account of my feelings to this elder of the church and to the other member who was with him, this young man came into the office. I was sitting with my back toward the door and barely observed that he came in. He listened with astonishment to what I was saying, and the first I knew he partly fell upon the floor and cried out in the greatest agony of mind, "Pray for me!"

The elder of the church and the other member knelt down and began to pray for him, and when they had prayed, I prayed for him myself. Soon after this they all retired and left me alone.

The question then arose in my mind, "Why did Elder B—— laugh so? Did he think that I was under a delusion, or crazy?" This suggestion brought a kind of darkness over my mind, and I began to wonder whether it had been proper for me—such a sinner as I had been—to pray for that young man. A cloud seemed to shut in over me. I had no hold upon anything in which I could rest. After a little while I retired to bed, not distressed in mind but still at a loss to know what to make of my present state. Notwithstanding the baptism I had received, this temptation so obscured my view that I went to bed without feeling sure that my peace was made with God.

I soon fell asleep, but almost as soon awoke again because of the great flow of the love of God in my heart. I was so filled with love that I could not sleep. Soon I fell asleep again and awoke in the same manner. When I awoke, this temptation would return to me, and the love that seemed to be in my heart would lessen; but as soon as I was asleep, it was so warm within me that I would immediately awaken. Thus I continued until late in the night, when I finally obtained some sound sleep.

When I awoke in the morning the sun had risen and was pouring a clear light into my room. Words cannot express the impression that this sunlight made upon me. Instantly the baptism that I had received the night before returned upon me in the same manner. I arose upon my knees in the bed and wept aloud with joy, and remained for some time too much over-whelmed with the baptism of the Spirit to do anything but pour out my soul to God.

It seemed as if this morning's baptism was accompanied with a gentle reproof, and the Spirit seemed to say to me, "Will you doubt? Will you doubt?"

I cried, "No! I will not doubt. I cannot doubt!" He then cleared the subject up so much to my mind that it was in fact impossible for me to doubt that the Spirit of God had taken possession of my soul.

In this state I was taught the doctrine of justification by faith as a present experience. That doctrine had never taken possession of my mind. I had never viewed it distinctly as a fundamental doctrine of the Gospel. Indeed, I did not know at all what it meant in the proper sense. But I could now see and understand what was meant by the passage, "Being justified by faith, we have peace with God through our Lord Jesus Christ." I could see that the moment I believed, while up in the woods, all sense of condemnation had entirely dropped out of my mind, and that from that moment

I could not feel a sense of guilt or condemnation by any effort I could make. My sense of guilt was gone, my sins were gone, and I do not think I felt any more sense of guilt than if I never had sinned.

This was just the revelation I needed. I felt myself justified by faith, and, so far as I could see, I was in a state in which I did not sin. Instead of feeling that I was sinning all the time, my heart was so full of love that it overflowed. My cup ran over with blessing and with love. I could not feel that I was sinning against God, nor could I recover the least sense of guilt for my past sins. Of this experience of justification I said nothing to anybody at the time.

3

On this morning of which I have just spoken I went down into the office, and there I was having the renewal of these mighty waves of love and salvation flowing over me when Squire W—— came into the office. I said a few words to him on the subject of his salvation. He looked at me with astonishment but made no reply whatever that I remember. He dropped his head, and after standing a few minutes left the office. I thought no more of it then, but afterward found that the remark I made pierced him like a sword, and he did not recover from it till he was converted.

Soon after Squire W—— had left the office, Deacon B—— came into the office and said to me, "Mr. Finney, do you remember that my cause is to be tried at ten o'clock this morning? I suppose you are ready?" I had been retained to attend this suit as his attorney.

I replied to him, "Deacon B——, I have a retainer from the Lord Jesus Christ to plead his cause and I cannot plead yours."

He looked at me with astonishment and said, "What do you mean?"

I told him, in a few words, that I had enlisted in the cause of Christ, and then repeated that I had a retainer from the Lord Jesus Christ to plead his cause, and that he must go and get somebody else to attend his lawsuit. I could not do it.

He dropped his head and without making any reply went out. A few moments later, in passing the window, I observed that Deacon B — was standing in the road, seemingly lost in deep meditation. He went away, as I afterward learned, and immediately settled his suit privately. He then betook himself to prayer and soon got into a much higher religious state than he had ever been before.

I soon sallied forth from the office to converse with those whom I might meet about their souls. I had the impression, which has never left my mind, that God wanted me to preach the Gospel, and that I must begin immediately. I somehow seemed to know it. If you ask me how I knew it, I cannot tell how I knew it, anymore than I can tell how I knew that that was the love of God and the baptism of the Holy Spirit which I had received. I did somehow know it with a certainty that was past all possibility of doubt. And so I seemed to know that the Lord commissioned me to preach the Gospel.

When I was first convicted, the thought had occurred to my mind that if I was ever converted I should be obliged to leave my profession, of which I was very fond, and preach the Gospel. This at first stumbled me. I thought I had taken too many pains and spent too much time and study in my profession to think now of becoming a Christian, if by doing so I should be obliged to preach the Gospel. However, I at last came to the conclusion that I must submit that question to God. I had never begun the study of law from any regard to God, and I had no right to make any conditions with him. I therefore had laid aside the thought of becoming a minister until it was sprung in my mind, as I have related, on my way from my place of prayer in the woods.

But now after receiving these baptisms of the Spirit I was quite willing to preach the Gospel. Nay, I found that I was unwilling to do anything else. I had no longer any desire to practice law. Everything in that direction was shut up and had no longer any attractions for me at all. I had no desire to make money. I had no hungering and thirsting after worldly pleasures and amusements in any direction. My whole mind was taken up with Jesus and his salvation, and the world seemed to me of very little consequence. Nothing, it seemed to me, could compete with the worth of souls, and no labor, I thought, could be so sweet and no employment so exalted as that of holding up Christ to a dying world.

With this impression, as I said, I sallied forth to talk with any whom I might meet. I first dropped in at the shop of a shoemaker, who was a pious man and one of the most praying Christians, as I thought, in the church. I found him in conversation with a son of one of the elders of the church, and this young man was defending universal salvation. Mr. W——, the shoemaker, turned to me and said, "Mr. Finney, what do you think of the argument of this young man?" He then stated what he had been saying in defense of universalism. The answer appeared to me so ready that in a moment I was able to blow his argument to the wind.

The young man saw at once that his argument was gone, and he rose up without making any reply and went suddenly out. But soon I observed, as I stood in the middle of the room, that the young man, instead of going along the street, had passed around the shop, climbed over the fence and was steering straight across the fields toward the woods. I thought no more about it until evening when the young man came out and appeared to be a bright convert, giving the story of his experience. He said that he had gone into the woods and there given his heart to God.

I spoke with many persons that day, and I believe the Spirit of God made lasting impressions upon every one of them. I cannot remember one whom I spoke with, who was not soon after converted. Just at evening I called at the house of a friend where a young man lived who was employed in distilling whiskey. The family had heard that I had become a Christian and as they were about to sit down to tea, they urged me to sit down and take tea with them. The man of the house and his wife were both professing Christians. But a sister of the lady was present, an unconverted girl, and a young man, a distant relative of the family, who was a professed Universalist. He was rather an outspoken and talkative Universalist, a young man of a good deal of energy of character.

I sat down with them to tea and they requested me to ask a blessing. It was what I had never done, but I did not hesitate a moment and began to ask the blessing of God as we sat around the table. I had scarcely more than begun before the state of these young people rose before my mind and excited so much compassion that I burst into weeping and was unable to proceed. Everyone around the table sat speechless for a short time while I continued to weep. Soon the young man moved back from the table and rushed out of the room. He fled to his room and locked himself in, and was not seen again until the next morning, when he came out expressing a blessed hope in Christ. He has been for many years an able minister of the Gospel.

In the course of the day a good deal of excitement was created in the village because of what the Lord had done for my soul. Some thought one thing and some another. At evening, without any appointment having been made, I observed that the people were going to the place where they usually held their conference and prayer meetings. My conversion had created a good deal of astonishment in the village. I afterward learned that some time before this some members of the church had proposed in a church meeting to make me a particular subject of prayer, but that Mr. Gale had discouraged them, saying that he did not believe I would ever be converted. From talking with me he told them he had found that I was very much enlightened upon the subject of religion but very much hardened. And furthermore, he said he was almost discouraged, because I led the choir and taught the young people sacred music. They were so much under my influence that he did not believe they would ever be converted while I remained in Adams.

I found after I was converted that some of the wicked men in the place had hidden behind me. One in particular, a Mr. C——, who had a pious wife, had repeatedly said to her, "If religion is true, why don't you convert Finney? If you Christians can convert Finney, I will believe in religion."

An old lawyer by the name of M——, living in Adams, when he heard it rumored that day that I was converted said that it was all a hoax and that I was simply trying to see what I could make Christian people believe.

However, with one consent the people seemed to rush to the place of worship. I went there myself. The minister was there, and nearly all the principal people in the village. No one seemed ready to open the meeting, but the house was packed to its utmost capacity. I did not wait for anybody, but rose and began by saying that I then knew that religion was from God. I went on and told such parts of my experience as it seemed important for me to tell.

This Mr. C——, who had promised his wife that if I was converted he would believe in religion, was present. Mr. M——, the old lawyer, was also present. What the Lord enabled me to say seemed to take a wonderful hold upon the people. Mr. C—— got up, pressed through the crowd, and went home, leaving his hat. Mr. M—— also left and went home, saying I was crazy. "He is in earnest," said he; "there is no mistake, but he is deranged, that is clear."

As soon as I had finished speaking, Mr. Gale, the minister, rose and made a confession. He said he believed he had been in the way of the church, and then confessed that he had discouraged the church when they had proposed to pray for me. He said also that when he had heard the day that I was converted, he had promptly said that he did not believe it. He said he had no faith. He spoke in a very humble manner.

I had never made a prayer in public. But soon after Mr. Gale was through speaking, he called on me to pray. I did so, and think I had a good deal of enlargement and liberty in prayer. We had a wonderful meeting that evening, and from that day we had a meeting every evening for a long time. The work spread on every side.

As I had been a leader among the young people I immediately appointed a meeting for them, which they all attended—that is, all of the class with which I was acquainted. I gave up my time to labor for their conversion, and the Lord blessed every effort that was made in a very wonderful manner. They were converted one after another with great rapidity, and the work continued among them until only one of their number was left unconverted.

The work spread among all classes and extended itself not only through the village but also out of the village in every direction. My heart was so full that for more than a week I did not feel at all inclined to sleep or eat. I seemed literally to have meat to eat that the world knew nothing of. I did not feel the need of food or of sleep. My mind was full and overflowing with the love of God. I went on in this way for a good many days until I found that I must rest and sleep. From that point I was more cautious in my labors, and ate regularly and slept as much as I could.

The Word of God had wonderful power, every day and I was surprised to find that a few words spoken to an individual would stick in his heart like an arrow.

After a short time I went down to Henderson to visit my father. He was an unconverted man. Only one of the family, my youngest brother, had ever made a profession of faith in Christ. My father met me at the gate and said, "How do you do, Charles?"

I replied, "I am well, Father, body and soul. But, Father, you are an old man. All your children are grown up and have left your house, and I never heard a prayer in my father's house."

Father dropped his head, burst into tears and replied, "I know it, Charles. Come in and pray yourself."

We went in and engaged in prayer. My father and mother were greatly moved, and in a very short time thereafter they were both converted. I do not know but that my mother had had a secret hope before, but if so none of the family ever knew it.

I remained in that neighborhood for two or three days and conversed with such people as I could meet with. I believe it was the next Monday night that they had a monthly united meeting of prayer in that town. There was a Baptist church there that had a minister, and a small Congregational church without a minister. The town was very much of a moral waste however, and at this time religion was at a very low ebb.

My youngest brother attended this monthly meeting of which I have spoken, and afterward gave me an account of it. The Baptists and Congregationalists were in the habit of holding a united monthly meeting. But few attended, and therefore it was held at a private house. On this occasion they met as usual in the parlor of a private house. A few of the members of the Baptist church and a few Congregationalists were present.

The deacon of the Congregational church was a spare, feeble old man by the name of M——. He was quiet in his ways and had a good reputation for piety, but he seldom said much upon the subject. He was a good specimen of a New England deacon. He was present, and they called upon him to lead the meeting. He read a passage of scripture according to their custom. They then sang a hymn, and Deacon M—— stood up behind his chair and led in prayer. The other persons present, all of them professing Christians and younger than he, knelt down around the room.

My brother said that Deacon M—— began as usual in his prayer in a low, feeble voice but soon began to wax warm and to raise his voice, which became tremulous with emotion. He proceeded to pray with more and more earnestness until soon he began to rise upon his toes and come down upon his heels, and then to rise upon his toes and drop upon his heels again, so that they could feel the jar in the room. He continued to raise his voice and to rise upon his toes and come down upon his heels more emphatically. And as the spirit of prayer led him onward, he began to raise his chair together with his heels, and bring that down upon the floor. Soon he raised it a little higher and brought it down with still more emphasis. He continued to do this, and grew more and more engaged, until he would bring the chair down as if he would break it to pieces.

In the meantime the brothers and sisters that were on their knees began to groan, and sigh, and weep, and agonize in prayer. The deacon continued to struggle until he was about exhausted. When he ceased, my brother said that no one in the room could get off his knees. They could only weep and confess and all melt down before the Lord. From this meeting the work of the Lord spread forth in every direction all over the town. And thus it spread at that time from Adams as a center throughout nearly all the towns in the county.

4

I have spoken of the conviction of Squire W——, in whose office I studied law. I have also said that when I was converted, it was in a grove where I went to pray. Very soon after my conversion, several other cases of conversion occurred that were reported to have taken place under similar circumstances, that is, persons went up into the grove to pray, and there made their peace with God.

When Squire W—— heard them tell their experiences, one after the other, in our meetings, he thought that he had a parlor to pray in and that he was not going up into the woods to have the same story to tell that had been so often told. To this he strongly committed himself. Although this was a thing entirely immaterial in itself, yet it was a point on which his pride had become committed, and therefore he could not get into the kingdom of God.

I have found in my ministerial experience a great many cases of this kind, whereupon some question, perhaps immaterial in itself, a sinner's pride of heart would commit him. In all such cases the dispute must be yielded, or the sinner never will get into the kingdom of God. I have known persons to remain for weeks in great tribulation of mind, pressed by the Spirit, but they could make no progress until the point upon which they were committed was yielded. Squire W—— was the first case of the kind that ever come to my attension.

After he was converted, he said the question had frequently come up when he was in prayer, and that he had been made to see that it was pride that made him take that stand, and that kept him out of the kingdom of God. But still he had not been willing to admit this, even to himself. He tried in every way to make himself believe, and to make God believe, that he was not proud. One night, he said, he prayed all night in his parlor that God would have mercy on him, but in the morning he felt more distressed than ever. He finally became enraged that God did not hear his prayer and was tempted to kill himself. He was so tempted to use his pen-knife for that purpose that he actually threw it as far as he could, that it might be lost so that this temptation should not prevail.

He said that one night on returning from a meeting he was so pressed with a sense of his pride, and with the fact that it prevented his going up into the woods to pray, that he was determined to make himself believe, and make God believe that he was not proud. He looked around for a mud puddle in which to kneel down, that he might demonstrate that it was not pride which kept him from going into the woods. Thus he continued to struggle for several weeks.

But one afternoon I was sitting in our office with two of the elders of the church when the young man I had met at the shoemaker's shop came hastily into the office and exclaimed as he came, "Squire W—— is converted!" and proceeded to say: "I went up into the woods to pray, and heard someone over in the valley shouting very loud. I went up to the brow of the hill, where I could look down, and I saw Squire W—— pacing to and fro, and singing as loud as he could sing, and every few minutes he would stop and clap his hands with his full strength, and shout, 'I will rejoice in the

God of my salvation!' Then he would march and sing again, and then stop, and shout, and clap his hands."

While the young man was telling us this, behold, Squire W——appeared in sight, coming over the hill. As he came down to the foot of the hill we observed that he met Father T——, as we all called him, an aged Methodist brother. He rushed up to him, and took him right up in his arms. After setting him down and conversing a moment, he came rapidly toward the office.

When he came in, he was in profuse perspiration (he was a heavy man) and he cried out, "I've got it! I've got it!" clapped his hands with all his might, and fell upon his knees and began to give thanks to God. He then gave us an account of what had been passing in his mind and why he had not obtained a hope before. He said as soon as he gave up that point and went into the woods, his mind was relieved, and when he knelt down to pray, the Spirit of God came upon him and filled him with such unspeakable joy that it resulted in the scene which the young man witnessed. Of course from that time Squire W—— took a decided stand for God.

Toward spring the zeal of the older members of the church began to lessen. I had been in the habit of rising early in the morning and spending a season of prayer alone in the meeting-house, and I finally succeeded in interesting a considerable number of brothers to meet me there in the morning for a prayer meeting. This was at a very early hour, and we were generally together long before it was light enough to see to read. I persuaded my minister to attend these morning meetings.

But soon they began to be remiss; whereupon I would get up in time to go around to their houses and wake them up. Many times I went round and round and called the brothers whom I thought would be most likely to attend, and we would have a precious season of prayer. But still I found that they attended with more and more reluctance, which fact greatly tried me.

One morning I had been around in this way but when I returned to the meeting house only a few of them were there. Mr. Gale, my minister, was standing at the door of the church, and as I came up, all at once the glory of God shone upon and round about me in a manner most marvelous. The day was just beginning to dawn. But all at once a light perfectly glorious shone in my soul that almost prostrated me to the ground. In this light it seemed as if I could see that all nature except man praised and worshipped God. This light seemed to be like the brightness of the sun in every direction. It was too intense for the eyes. I remember casting my eyes down and breaking into a flood of tears because mankind did not praise God. I think I knew something then, by actual experience, of that light that prostrated Paul on his way to Damascus. It was surely a light such as I could not have endured long.

When I burst out into such loud weeping, Mr. Gale said, "What is the matter, brother Finney?"

I could not tell him. I found that he had seen no light and that he saw no reason why I should be in such a state of mind. I therefore said but little. I believe I merely replied that I saw the glory of God, and that I could not endure to think of the manner in which he was treated by men. Indeed it did not seem to me at the time that the vision of his glory which I had was to be described in words. I wept it out, and the vision, if it may be so called, passed away and left my mind calm.

When I was a young Christian, I used to have many seasons of communing with God which cannot be described in words. Not infrequently those seasons would end in an impression on my mind like this: "Go, see that you tell no man." I did not understand this at the time, and several times I paid no attention to this injunction but tried to tell my Christian friends what seasons of communion I had with him. But I soon found that it would not do to tell what was passing between the Lord and my soul. They could not understand it. They would look surprised and sometimes, I thought, incredulous. I soon learned to keep quiet in regard to those divine manifestations and say but little about them.

I used to spend a great deal of time in prayer, sometimes literally praying "without ceasing." I also found it very profitable, and felt very much inclined to hold frequent days of private fasting. On those days I would seek to be entirely alone with God—and would generally wander off into the woods, or get into the meeting house, or somewhere away entirely by myself.

Sometimes I would pursue a wrong course in fasting and attempt to examine myself according to the ideas of self-examination then entertained by my minister and the church. I would try to look into my own heart in the sense of examining my feelings, and would turn my attention particularly to my motives and the state of my mind. When I pursued this course, I found invariably that the day would close without any perceptible advance being made. Afterwards I saw clearly why this was so. Turning my attention, as I did, from the Lord Jesus Christ and looking into myself, examining my motives and feelings, my feelings all subsided.

But whenever I fasted and let the Spirit take his own course with me, and gave myself up to let him lead and instruct me, I always found it in the highest degree useful. I found I could not live without enjoying the presence of God, and if at any time a cloud came over me, I could not rest, I could not study, I could not attend to anything with the least satisfaction or benefit until the way was again cleared between my soul and God.

I had been very fond of my legal profession. But as I have said, when I was converted all was dark in that direction, and I had no longer any pleasure in attending to law business. I had many pressing invitations to conduct lawsuits, but I uniformly refused. I did not dare to trust myself in the excitement of a contested lawsuit; furthermore, the business of conducting other people's controversies appeared odious and offensive to me.

In those early days of my Christian experience, the Lord taught me many very important truths in regard to the spirit of prayer. Not long after I was converted a woman with whom I had boarded (though I did not board with her at this time) was taken very sick. She was not a Christian, but her husband was a professing Christian. He came into our office one evening, being a brother of Squire W——, and said to me, "My wife cannot live through the night."

The burden of prayer almost crushed me, the nature of which I could not at all understand, but with it came an intense desire to pray for that woman. The burden was so great that I left the office almost immediately and went up to the meeting house to pray for her. There I struggled, but I could not say much. I could only groan with groanings loud and deep.

I stayed a considerable time in the church in this state of mind, but I got no relief. I returned to the office, but I could not sit still. I could only walk the room and agonize. I returned to the meeting house again and went through the same process of struggling. For a long time I tried to get my prayer before the Lord, but somehow the words could not express it. I could only groan and weep without being able to express what I wanted in words. I returned to the office again and still found that I was unable to rest, and I returned

a third time to the meeting house. At this time the
Lord gave me power to prevail. I was enabled to roll
the burden upon him, and I obtained the assurance
in my own mind that the woman would not die, and
indeed that she would never die in her sins.

I returned to the office. My mind was perfectly quiet
and I soon left and retired to rest. Early the next morning the husband of this woman came into the office.
I inquired how his wife was. Smiling, he said, "She's
alive, and to all appearance better this morning."

I replied, "Brother W——, she will not die with
this sickness; you may rely upon it. And she will never
die in her sins." I do not know how I was made sure
of this, but it was in some way made plain to me so
that I had no doubt that she would recover. She did
recover and soon after obtained a hope in Christ.

At first I did not understand what this exercise of
mind was that I had passed through. But shortly after
in relating it to a Christian brother he said to me,
"Why, that was the travail of your soul." A few minutes'
conversation, and pointing me to certain scriptures,
gave me to understand what it was.

Another experience which I had soon after this
illustrates the same truth. I have spoken of one young
woman as belonging to the class of young people of
my acquaintance who remained unconverted. This attracted a good deal of attention and there was considerable conversation among Christians about her
case. She was a charming girl and very much enlightened on the subject of religion, but she remained in
her sins.

One of the elders of the church and myself agreed
to make her a daily subject of prayer, to continue to
present her case at the throne of grace, morning,
noon, and evening, until she was either converted, or
should die, or we should be unable to keep our covenant.
I found my mind greatly exercised about her as I con-

tinued to pray for her. I soon found, however, that the elder who had entered into this arrangement with me was losing the spirit of prayer for her. This did not discourage me. I continued to hold on with increasing importunity. I also availed myself of every opportunity to converse plainly and searchingly with her on the subject of her salvation.

After I had continued in this way for some time, one evening I called to see her just as the sun was setting. As I came up to the door I heard a shriek from a female voice and a scuffling and confusion inside the door. I stood and waited for the confusion to cease. The lady of the house soon came and opened the door. She held in her hand a portion of a book which had been torn in two. She was pale and very agitated. She held out that portion of the book which she had in her hand and said, "Mr. Finney, don't you think my sister has become a Universalist?"

The book was a defense of universal salvation. She had discovered her sister reading it in private and had tried to get it away from her. It was the struggle to obtain that book which I had heard.

I received this information at the door; whereupon I declined to go in. It struck me very much in the same way as the announcement about the sick woman already mentioned. It loaded me down with great agony. As I returned to my room, at some distance from that house, I felt almost as if I should stagger under the burden that was on my mind. I struggled, and groaned, and agonized, but could not present the case before God in words—only in groans and tears.

The discovery that that young woman, instead of being converted, was becoming convinced of universal salvation so astounded me that I could not break through with my faith and get hold of God in reference to her case. There seemed to be a darkness hanging over the question, as if a cloud had risen up between me and God in regard to prevailing for her salvation. But still the Spirit struggled within me with groanings that could not be uttered.

However, I was obliged to retire that night without having prevailed. But as soon as it was light I awoke, and the first thought that I had was to beseech the God of grace again for that young woman. I immediately arose and fell upon my knees. No sooner was I upon my knees than the darkness gave way and the whole subject opened to my mind, and as soon as I pled for her God said to me, "Yes! Yes!" If he had spoken with an audible voice, it would not have been more distinctly understood than was this word spoken within my soul. It instantly relieved all my concern for her. My mind became filled with the greatest peace and joy, and I felt a complete certainty that her salvation was secure.

I drew a false inference, however, in regard to the time, which indeed was not a thing particularly impressed upon my mind at the time of my prayer. I expected her to be converted immediately, but she was not. She remained in her sins for several months. I felt disappointed at the time that she was not converted at once, and was somewhat staggered about the question of whether I had really prevailed with God in her behalf.

Soon after I was converted, the man with whom I had been boarding for some time, who was a magistrate and one of the principal men in the place, was deeply convicted of sin. He had been elected a member of the legislature of the state. I was praying daily for him and urging him to give his heart to God. His conviction became very deep; but still, from day to day, he deferred submission and did not obtain a hope. My concern for him increased.

One afternoon several of his political friends had a lengthy interview with him. On the evening of the same day I attempted again to carry his case to God, as the urgency in my mind for his conversion had become very great. In my prayer I had drawn very near to God. I do not remember ever having been in more intimate communion with the Lord Jesus Christ than I was at that time. Indeed, his presence was so real that I was bathed in tears of joy and gratitude and love, and in this state of mind I attempted to pray for this friend.

But the moment I did so, my mouth was shut. I found it impossible to pray a word for him. The Lord seemed to say to me, "No, I will not hear." As anguish seized upon me, I thought at first it was a temptation. But the door was shut in my face. It seemed as if the Lord said to me, "Speak no more to me of that matter." It pained me beyond expression. I did not know what to make of it.

The next morning I saw him, and as soon as I brought up the question of submission to God he said to me, "Mr. Finney, I shall have nothing more to do with it until I return from the legislature. I stand committed to my political friends to carry out certain measures in the legislature that are incompatible with my first becoming a Christian and I have promised that I will not attend to the subject until after I have returned from Albany."

From the moment of that exercise the evening before, I had no spirit of prayer for him at all. As soon as he told me what he had done, I understood it. I could see that his convictions were all gone and that the Spirit of God had left him. From that time he grew more careless and hardened than ever.

When the time arrived he went to the legislature, and in the spring he returned an almost insane Universalist. I say almost insane, because, instead of having formed his opinions of universal salvation from any evidence or course of argument, he told me this:

"I have come to that conclusion, not because I have found it taught in the Bible, but because such a doctrine is so opposed to the carnal mind. It is a doctrine so generally rejected and spoken against as to prove that it is distasteful to the carnal, or unconverted mind." This was astonishing to me. But everything else that I could get out of him was as wild and absurd as this. He remained in his sins, finally fell into decay, and died at last, as I have been told, a dilapidated man.

5

I have said that in the spring of the year the older members of the church began to decline in their engagedness and zeal for God. This greatly oppressed me, as it did also the young converts generally. About this time I read in a newspaper an article entitled "A Revival Revived." The substance of it was that in a certain place there had been a revival during the winter, but in the spring it declined; yet upon earnest prayer being offered for the continued outpouring of the Spirit, the revival was powerfully revived. This article set me into a flood of weeping.

I was at that time boarding with Mr. Gale and I took the article to him. I was so overcome with a sense of the divine goodness in hearing and answering prayer, and with a felt assurance that he would hear and answer prayer for the revival of his work in Adams, that I went through the house weeping aloud like a child. Mr. Gale seemed surprised at my feelings and my expressed confidence that God would revive his work. The article made no such impression on him.

At the next meeting of the young people I proposed that we should observe fixed times for secret prayer for the revival of God's work; that we should pray at sunrise, at noon, and at sunset, in our closets, and continue this for one week, when we would come together again and see what further was to be done.

No other means were used for the revival of God's work. But the spirit of prayer was immediately poured out wonderfully upon the young converts. Before the week was out I learned that some of them, when they would attempt to observe this season of prayer, would lose all their strength and, unable to rise to their feet or even stand upon their knees in their closets, would lie prostrate on the floor and pray with unutterable groanings for the outpouring of the Spirit of God.

The Spirit was poured out and before the week ended all the meetings were thronged. There was as much interest in religion as there had been at any time during the revival.

And here a mistake was made, or perhaps I should say, a sin committed, by some of the older members of the church, which resulted in great evil. As I afterward learned, a considerable number of the older people resisted this new movement among the young converts. They were jealous of it. They did not know what to make of it and felt that the young converts were getting out of their place in being so forward and so urgent upon the older members of the church. This state of mind finally grieved the Spirit of God. It was not long before alienations began to arise among these older members of the church, which finally resulted in great evil to those who had allowed themselves to resist this latter revival.

The young people held out well. The converts were almost universally sound and have been thoroughly efficient Christians.

In the spring of this year, 1822, I put myself under the care of the presbytery as a candidate for the gospel ministry. Some of the ministers urged me to go to Princeton to study theology, but I declined. When they asked me why I would not go to Princeton, I told them that my financial circumstances forbade it. This was true, but they said they would see that my expenses were paid. Still I refused to go and when urged to give them my reasons, I plainly told them that I would not put myself under such an influence as they had been under. I was confident that they had been wrongly educated and were not ministers that met my ideal of what a minister of Christ should be. I told them this reluctantly, but I could not honestly withhold it. So they appointed my pastor to superintend my studies. He offered me the use of his library and said he would give what attention I needed to my theological studies.

But my studies, so far as he was concerned as my teacher, were little else than controversy. I could not receive his views on the subject of atonement, regeneration, faith, repentance, the slavery of the will, or any of the kindred doctrines. But of these views he was quite tenacious, and he seemed sometimes not a little impatient because I did not receive them without question. He used to tell me that if I insisted on reasoning on these subjects, I would probably land in infidelity. He furthermore warned me repeatedly, and very feelingly, that as a minister I would never be useful unless I embraced the truth, meaning the truth as he believed and taught it.

I am sure I was quite willing to believe what I found taught in the Bible, and told him so. We used to have many protracted discussions, and I would often come from his study greatly depressed and discouraged, saying to myself, "I cannot embrace these views come what will. I cannot believe they are taught in the Bible." Several times I was on the point of giving up study for the ministry altogether.

There was but one member of the church to whom I opened my mind freely on this subject, and that was Elder H——, a very godly, praying man. He had been educated in Princeton views, and held pretty strongly the higher doctrines of Calvinism. Nevertheless, as we had frequent and protracted conversations, he became satisfied that I was right. He would call on me frequently to have seasons of prayer with me, to strengthen me in my studies and in my discussions with Mr. Gale, and to convince me more and more firmly that, come what would, I would preach the Gospel.

Several times he happened to meet me when I was in a state of great depression, after coming from Mr. Gale's study. At such times he would go with me to my room, and sometimes we would continue until a late hour at night crying to God for light and strength and for faith to accept and do his perfect will. He lived more than three miles from the village, and frequently he stayed with me until ten or eleven o'clock at night, and then walked home. The dear old man! I have reason to believe that he prayed for me daily as long as he lived.

After I got into the ministry and great opposition was raised to my preaching, I met Elder H—— one time and he alluded to the opposition. "Oh!" he said, "my soul is so burdened that I pray for you day and night. But I am sure that God will help. Go on," he said, "go on, brother Finney. The Lord will give you deliverance."

After many discussions with Mr. Gale in pursuing my theological studies, the presbytery was finally called together at Adams to examine me, and, if they could agree to do so, to license me to preach the Gospel. This was in March, 1824. I expected a severe struggle with them in my examination, but I found them a good deal softened. The evident blessing that had attended my conversations, and my teaching in prayer and conference meetings, and in these lectures of which I have spoken, rendered them more cautious than they would otherwise have been in getting into any controversy with me. In the course of my examination they avoided asking any such questions as would naturally bring my views into collision with theirs.

When they had examined me, they voted unanimously to license me to preach. Unexpectedly they asked me if I received the confession of faith of the Presbyterian church. I had not examined the large work containing the catechism and confession. This had not been a part of my study. I replied that I received it for substance of doctrine, so far as I understood it. But I spoke in a way that plainly implied that I did not pretend to know much about it. However, I answered honestly, as I understood it at the time. They heard the trial sermons which I had written, on texts which had been given me by the presbytery, and went through with all the ordinary details of such an examination.

At this meeting of presbytery I first saw Rev. Daniel Nash, who is generally known as "Father Nash." He was a member of the presbytery. A large congregation was assembled to hear my examination. I got in a little late and saw a man standing in the pulpit speaking to the people, as I supposed. He looked at me as I came in and was looking at others as they passed up the aisles.

As soon as I reached my seat and listened, I observed that he was praying. I was surprised to see him looking all over the house, as if he were talking to the people, while in fact he was praying to God. Of course it did not sound to me much like prayer, and he was at that time indeed in a very cold and backslidden state. I shall have occasion frequently to mention him hereafter.

The next Sunday after I was licensed I preached for Mr. Gale. When I came out of the pulpit he said to me, "Mr. Finney, I shall be very much ashamed to have it known, wherever you go, that you studied theology with me." This was so much like him, and like what he had repeatedly said to me, that I made little or no reply to it. I held down my head, feeling discouraged, and went my way.

Afterward he viewed this subject very differently, and told me that he blessed the Lord that in all our discussion, and in all he had said to me, he had not had the least influence to change my views. He very frankly confessed his error in the manner in which he had dealt with me, and said that if I had listened to him I would have been ruined as a minister.

The fact is that Mr. Gale's education for the ministry had been entirely defective. He had imbibed a set of opinions, both theological and practical, that were a straitjacket to him. He could accomplish very little or nothing if he carried out his own principles. I had the use of his library, and searched it thoroughly on all the questions of theology which came up for examination, and the more I examined the books, the more dissatisfied I became.

I had been used to the close and logical reasonings of the judges as I found them reported in our law works; but when I went to Mr. Gale's old school library, I found almost nothing proved to my satisfaction. I am sure it was not because I was opposed to the truth but because the positions of these theological authors were unsound and not satisfactorily sustained. They often seemed to me to state one thing and prove another, and frequently fell short of logically proving anything.

Often when I left Mr. Gale I would go to my room and spend a long time on my knees over my Bible. Indeed, I read my Bible on my knees a great deal during those days of conflict, beseeching the Lord to teach me his own mind on those points. I had nowhere to go but directly to the Bible and to the philosophy or workings of my own mind as revealed in consciousness.

My views slowly took on a positive type. At first I found myself unable to receive his peculiar views.

Then gradually I formed views of my own in opposition to them, which appeared to me to be unequivocally taught in the Bible.

But there was another defect in brother Gale's education which I regarded as fundamental. If he had ever been converted to Christ, he had failed to receive that divine anointing of the Holy Spirit that would make him a power in the pulpit and in society for the conversion of souls. He had fallen short of receiving the baptism of the Holy Spirit, which is indispensable to ministerial success.

When Christ commissioned his apostles to go and preach, he told them to abide at Jerusalem until they were endued with power from on high. This power, as everyone knows, was the baptism of the Holy Spirit poured out upon them on the day of Pentecost. This was an indispensable qualification for success in their ministry. I did not suppose then, nor do I now, that this baptism was simply the power to work miracles. The power to work miracles and the gift of tongues were given as signs to attest the reality of their divine commission.

But the baptism itself was a divine purifying, an anointing bestowing on them a divine illumination, filling them with faith and love, with peace and power, so that their words were made sharp in the hearts of God's enemies, quick and powerful, like a two-edged sword. This is an indispensable qualification of a successful ministry, and I have often been surprised and pained that to this day so little stress is laid upon this qualification for preaching Christ to a sinful world. Without the direct teaching of the Holy Spirit a man will never make much progress in preaching the Gospel. The fact is, unless he can preach the Gospel as an experience, present Christ to mankind as a matter of personal encounter, his speculations and theories will come far short of preaching the Gospel.

I have said that Mr. Gale afterward concluded that he had not been converted. That he was a sincere, good man, in the sense of honestly holding his opinions, I do not doubt. But he was sadly defective in his education theologically, philosophically and practically, and so far as I could learn his spiritual state, he did not have the peace of the Gospel when I sat under his ministry.

Let not the reader, from anything that I have said, supposed that I did not love Mr. Gale and highly respect him. I did both. He and I remained the firmest friends to the day of his death. I have said what I have in relation to his views because I think it applicable to many of the ministers even of the present day. I think that their practical views of preaching the Gospel, whatever their theological views may be, are very defective indeed, and that their want of the anointing and power of the Holy Spirit is a radical defect in their preparation for the ministry. I say this not censoriously, but still I would record it as a fact which has long been settled in my mind, and over which I have long had occasion to mourn. And as I have become more and more acquainted with the ministry in this and other countries, I am persuaded that with all the training, discipline and education, there is a lack in practical views of the best way of presenting the Gospel to men and in adapting means to secure results. I have noticed especially a lack in their lives of the power of the Holy Spirit.

6

Having had no regular training for the ministry I did not expect or desire to labor in large towns or cities or minister to cultivated congregations. I intended to go into the new settlements and preach in schoolhouses, barns and groves, as best I could. Accordingly, soon after being licensed to preach, for the sake of being introduced to the region where I proposed to labor, I took a commission for six months from a missionary society located in Oneida County. I went into the northern part of Jefferson County and began my labors at Evans' Mills, near the town of Le Ray.

At this place I found two churches, a small Congregational church without a minister and a Baptist church with a minister. I presented my credentials to the deacons of the church. They were very glad to see me and I soon began my labors. They had no meeting house, but the two churches worshipped alternately in a large stone schoolhouse, large enough to accommodate all the children in the village. The Baptists occupied the house one Sunday and the Congregationalists the next, so that I could have the house only every other Sunday, but could use it evenings as often as I pleased. I therefore divided my Sundays between Evans' Mills and Antwerp, a village some sixteen or eighteen miles still farther north.

I began to preach in the stone schoolhouse at Evans'

Mills. The people were very much interested and thronged the place to hear me preach. They praised my preaching, and the little Congregational church became very much interested, hopeful that they would be built up and that there would be a revival. Convictions of a few occurred under nearly every sermon that I preached, but still no general conviction appeared upon the public mind.

I was very much dissatisfied with this state of things, and at one of my evening services, after having preached there two or three Sundays and several evenings in the week, I told the people at the close of my sermon that I had come there to secure the salvation of their souls. My preaching, I knew, was highly complimented by them, but after all, I did not come there to please them but to bring them to repentance. It mattered not to me how well my preaching pleased them if they rejected my Master. Something was wrong, either in me or in them, for the kind of interest they manifested in my preaching was doing them no good. I could not spend my time with them unless they were going to receive the Gospel.

I then, quoting the words of Abraham's servant, said to them, "Now will you deal kindly and truly with my master? If you will, tell me; and if not, tell me, that I may turn to the right hand or to the left." I turned this question over and pressed it upon them, insisting that I must know what course they proposed to pursue. If they did not purpose to become Christians and enlist in the service of the Savior, I wanted to know so that my labor with them would not be in vain. I said to them, "You admit that what I preach is the Gospel. You profess to believe it. Now will you receive it? Do you mean to receive it, or do you intend to reject it? You must have some mind about it. And now I have a right to take it for granted, inasmuch as you admit that I have preached the truth, that you acknowledge your obligation at once to become Christians. This obligation you do not deny. But will you meet this obligation? Will you discharge it? Will you do what you admit you ought to do? If you will not, tell me, and if you will, tell me, that I may turn to the right hand or to the left."

After turning this over until I saw they understood it well, and looked greatly surprised at my manner of putting it, I then said to them, "Now I must know your minds, and I want you who have made up your minds to become Christians and give your pledge to make your peace with God immediately, to rise up. On the contrary, those of you who are resolved that you will not become Christians and wish me so to understand, and wish Christ so to understand, are to sit still."

After making this plain so that I knew that they understood it, I then said: "You who are now willing to pledge to me and to Christ that you will immediately make your peace with God, please rise up. On the contrary, you who are committed to remain in your present attitude, not to accept Christ, may sit still." They looked at one another and at me, and all sat still, just as I expected.

After looking at them for a few moments, I said, "Then you are committed. You have taken your stand. You have rejected Christ and his Gospel, and you are witnesses one against the other and God is witness against you all. This is explicit, and you may remember as long as you live that you have thus publicly committed yourselves against the Savior and said, 'We will not have this man, Christ Jesus, to reign over us.' "

When I thus pressed them they began to look angry and rose *en masse* and started for the door. When they began to move, I paused. As soon as I stopped speaking they turned to see why I did not go on. I said, "I am sorry for you, and will preach to you once more, the Lord willing, tomorrow night."

They all left the house except Deacon McC—— who was a deacon of the Baptist church in that place. I saw that the Congregationalists were confounded. They were few in number and very weak in faith. I presume that every member of both churches who was present, except Deacon McC——, was taken aback, and concluded that the matter was all over, that by my imprudence I had dashed and ruined all hopeful appearances.

Deacon McC—— came up and took me by the hand and smiling said, "Brother Finney, you have got them. They cannot rest under this; rely upon it. The brethren are all discouraged," said he, "but I am not. I believe you have done the very thing that needed to be done and that we will see the results."

I thought so myself, of course. I intended to place them in a position which, upon reflection, would make them tremble in view of what they had done. All that evening and the next day they were full of wrath. Deacon McC—— and myself agreed to spend the next day in fasting and prayer—separately in the morning, and together in the afternoon.

I learned in the course of the day that the people were threatening to ride me on a rail, to tar and feather me, and to give me a walking paper. Some of them cursed me and said that I had put them under oath and made them swear that they would not serve God. They said that I had drawn them into a solemn and public pledge to reject Christ and his Gospel. This was no more than I expected.

In the afternoon Deacon McC—— and I went into a grove together and spent the whole afternoon in prayer. Just at evening the Lord gave us great enlargement and promise of victory. Both of us felt assured that we had prevailed with God, and that the power of God would be revealed among the people that night.

As the time came for meeting we left the woods

and went to the village. The people were already throng-
ing to the place of worship. Those who had not already
gone, seeing us go through the village, turned out of
their stores and places of business, or threw down their
ball clubs where they were playing upon the green,
and packed the house to its utmost capacity.

I had not taken a thought with regard to what I
should preach. Indeed, this was common with me at
that time. The Holy Spirit was upon me, and I felt
confident that when the time came for action I would
know what to preach. As soon as I found the house
packed so that no more could get in, I arose, and without
any formal introduction of singing I began with these
words: "Say to the righteous that it shall be well
with him, for they shall eat the fruit of their doings.
Woe to the wicked! it shall be ill with him; for the
reward of his hands shall be given him."

The Spirit of God came upon me with such power
that it was like opening a battery upon them. For more
than an hour, and perhaps for an hour and a half,
the word of God came through me to them in a manner
that I could see was carrying all before it. It was a
fire and a hammer breaking the rock, and as a sword
that was piercing to the dividing asunder of soul and
spirit. I saw that a general conviction was spreading
over the whole congregation. Many of them could not
hold up their heads.

I did not call that night for any reversal of the action
they had taken the night before, nor for any committal
of themselves in any way, but took it for granted during
the whole of the sermon that they were committed
against the Lord. Then I appointed another meeting
and dismissed the congregation.

As the people withdrew I observed a woman in one
part of the house being supported in the arms of some
of her friends, and I went to see what was the matter,
supposing that she was in a fainting spell. I soon found

that she was not fainting but that she could not speak. There was a look of the greatest anguish in her face and she made me understand that she could not speak. I advised the women to take her home and pray with her to see what the Lord would do. They informed me that she was Miss G——, sister of the well-known missionary, and that she was a member of the church in good standing for several years.

That evening, instead of going to my usual lodgings, I accepted an invitation and went home with a family where I had not stopped overnight. Early in the morning I found that I had been sent for several times during the night, at the place where I was supposed to be, to visit families where there were persons under awful distress of mind. This led me to sally forth among the people, and everywhere I found a state of wonderful conviction of sin and alarm for their souls.

After lying in a speechless state about sixteen hours, Miss G——'s mouth was opened, and a new song was given her. She was taken from the horrible pit of miry clay, her feet were set upon a rock, and many saw it and feared. It occasioned a great searching among the members of the church. She declared that she had been entirely deceived. For eight years she had been a member of the church and thought she was a Christian, but during the sermon the night before she saw that she had never known the true God. When his character arose before her mind as it was then presented, her hope "perished," as she expressed it, "like a moth." She said such a view of the holiness of God was presented that like a great wave it swept her away from her standing and annihilated her hope in a moment.

I found at this place a number of deists, some of them men of high standing in the community. One of them was a keeper of a hotel in the village, and others were respectable men of more than average intelligence. But they seemed banded together to resist the revival. When I was certain of the ground they took, I preached a sermon to meet their wants, for on Sunday they came to hear me preach.

I took this for my text: "Suffer me a little, and I will show you that I have yet to speak on God's behalf. I will bring my knowledge from afar, and I will ascribe righteousness to my Maker." I went over the whole ground, so far as I understood their position, and God enabled me to sweep it clean.

As soon as I had finished and dismissed the meeting, the hotel keeper, who was the leader among them, came to me and taking me by the hand said, "Mr. Finney, I am convinced. You have met and answered all my difficulties. Now I want you to go home with me, for I want to converse with you."

I heard no more of their infidelity, and if I remember right, that class of men were nearly all converted.

There was one old man in this place who was not only an infidel but a great railer at religion. He was very angry at the revival movement. I heard every day of his railing and blaspheming, but I took no public notice of it. He refused altogether to attend a meeting. But in the midst of his opposition and when his excitement was great, while sitting one morning at the table he suddenly fell out of his chair in a fit of apoplexy. A physician was immediately called who, after a brief examination, told him that he could live but a very short time and that if he had anything to say he must say it at once. He had just strength and time to stammer out, "Don't let Finney pray over my corpse." This was the last of his opposition in that place.

At this place I again saw Father Nash, the man who prayed with his eyes open at the meeting of the presbytery when I was licensed. After he was at the presbytery he was taken with inflamed eyes and for several weeks was shut up in a dark room. He could neither read nor write and gave himself up almost entirely to prayer. He had a terrible overhauling in his whole Christian experience and as soon as he was able to see, with a double black veil before his face, he sallied forth to labor for souls.

When he came to Evans' Mills he was full of the power of prayer. He was another man altogether from what he had been at any former period of his Christian life. I found that he had "a praying list," as he called it, of the names of persons whom he made subjects of prayer every day and sometimes many times a day. Praying with him and hearing him pray in the meetings, I found that his gift of prayer was wonderful and his faith almost miraculous.

There was a man by the name of D—— who kept a low tavern in a corner of the village, whose house was the resort of all the opposers of the revival. The barroom was a place of blasphemy and he himself a most profane, ungodly, abusive man. He went railing about the streets in regard to the revival, and would take particular pains to swear and blaspheme whenever he saw a Christian. One of the young converts lived almost across the way from him, and he told me that he meant to sell and move out of that neighborhood because every time he was out of doors and D—— saw him, he would come out and swear, and curse, and say everything he could to wound his feelings. He had not been at any of our meetings. Of course he was ignorant of the great truths of religion and despised the whole Christian enterprise.

Father Nash heard us speak of this Mr. D—— as "a hard case," and immediately put his name upon his praying list. He remained in town a day or two and went on his way, having in view another field of labor.

Not many days afterward, as we were holding an evening meeting with a very crowded house, who should come in but this notorious D——? His entrance created a considerable movement in the congregation. People feared that he had come in to make a disturbance. The fear and abhorrence of him had become very general among Christians, so that when he came in some of the people got up and left. I knew his face and kept my eye on him.

I very soon became satisfied that he had not come in to oppose; rather, he was in great anguish of mind. He sat and writhed upon his seat and was very uneasy. He soon arose and tremblingly asked me if he might say a few words. I told him that he might. He then proceeded to make one of the most heartbroken confessions that I ever heard. His confession seemed to cover the whole ground of his treatment of God, of Christians, of the revival, and of everything good.

This thoroughly broke up the fallow ground in many hearts. It was the most powerful means that could have been used just then to give an impetus to the work. D—— soon came out and professed a hope in Christ, abolished all the revelry and profanity of his barroom, and as long as I stayed there, and I know not how much longer, a prayer meeting was held in his barroom nearly every night.

7

A little way from the village of Evans' Mills was a settlement of Germans where there was a German church with several elders and a considerable membership, but no minister and no regular religious meetings. Once each year they were in the habit of having a minister come up from the Mohawk Valley to administer the ordinances of baptism and the Lord's Supper. He would catechize their children and receive such of them as had made the required attainments in knowledge. This was the way in which they became Christians. They were required to commit to memory the catechism, and to be able to answer certain doctrinal questions; whereupon they were admitted to full communion in the church. After receiving the communion they took it for granted that they were Christians and that all was safe. This is the way in which that church had been organized.

But mingling as they did in the scenes that passed in the village, they requested me to go out there and preach. I consented, and the first time I preached I took this text: "Without holiness no man shall see the Lord."

The settlement turned out *en masse*, and the schoolhouse where they worshipped was filled to its utmost capacity. They could understand English well. I began by showing what holiness is not. Under this head I took everything that they considered to be religion and showed that it was not holiness at all. In the second place I showed what holiness is. Thirdly, I showed what is intended by seeing the Lord; and then, why those that had no holiness could never see the Lord— why they could never be admitted to his presence and be accepted of him. I concluded with such pointed remarks as were intended to make the subject go home. And it did go home by the power of the Holy Spirit. The sword of the Lord slew them on the right hand and on the left.

In a very few days it was found that the whole settlement was under conviction. Elders of the church and all were in the greatest consternation, feeling that they had no holiness. At their request I appointed a meeting for inquiry, to give instruction to inquirers. This was in their harvest time. I held the meeting at one o'clock in the afternoon and found the house literally packed. People had thrown down the implements with which they were gathering their harvest and had come into the meeting. As many were assembled as could be packed in the house.

I took a position in the center of the house, as I could not move around among them, asked them questions and encouraged them to ask questions. They became very interested and were very free in asking questions and in answering the questions which I asked them. I seldom ever attended a more interesting or profitable meeting than that.

I remember one woman who came in late and sat near the door. When I came to speak to her, I said, "You look unwell."

"Yes," she replied, "I am very sick. I have been in bed until I came to the meeting. But I cannot read, and I wanted to hear God's word so much that I got up and came to the meeting."

"How did you come?"

"I came on foot."

"How far is it?"

"We call it three miles," she said.

On inquiry I found that she was under conviction of sin, and had a most remarkably clear apprehension of her character and position before God. She was converted soon after, and a remarkable convert she was. My wife said that she was one of the most remarkable women in prayer that she ever heard pray and that she repeated more scripture in her prayers than any person she ever heard.

I addressed another, a tall dignified looking woman, and asked her what was the state of her mind. She replied immediately that she had given her heart to God, and went on to say that the Lord had taught her to read since she had learned how to pray. I asked her what she meant. She said she never could read, and never had known her letters. But when she gave her heart to God, she was greatly distressed because she could not read God's Word.

"But I thought," she said, "that Jesus could teach me to read, and I asked him if he would not please teach me to read his Word. I thought after I had prayed that I could read. The children have a Testament and I went and got it, and I thought I could read what I had heard them read. I went over to the school ma'am, and asked her if I read right, and she said I did. And ever since then I can read the Word of God for myself."

I said no more, but thought there must be some mistake, yet the woman appeared to be quite in earnest and quite intelligent in what she said. I took pains afterward to inquire of her neighbors. They affirmed that she had an excellent character, and that she could not read a syllable until after she was converted. I leave this to speak for itself. There is no use in theorizing. Such were the undoubted facts.

The revival among the Germans resulted in the conversion of the whole church and of nearly the whole community of Germans. It was one of the most interesting revivals that I ever witnessed.

I have only narrated some of the principal facts that I remember about this revival. But I would further say respecting it, that a great unity of feeling and a wonderful spirit of prayer prevailed among Christians. The little Congregational church, as soon as they saw the results of the next evening's preaching, recovered themselves, for they had been scattered, discouraged, and confounded the night before. They rallied and took hold of the work as best they could, and though a feeble and inefficient band, they grew in grace and in the knowledge of the Lord Jesus Christ during that revival.

The German woman of whom I have spoken as being sick when she came to the meeting of inquiry united with the Congregational church. A very affecting incident occurred at the time she gave testimony of her Christian experience. There was a mother in Israel belonging to that church, by the name of S——, a very godly woman, of ripe age and piety. We had been sitting for a long time listening to testimonies of those who came forward as candidates for admission to the church. At length this German woman arose and related her experience. It was one of the most touching, childlike, interesting Christian experiences that I ever listened to.

As she was going on with her narrative I observed that old Mrs. S—— rose up from her place, and as the house was filled, crowded her way around as best she could. At first I supposed she was going out doors. I was so occupied with the woman's narrative that I was barely conscious of Mrs. S——'s moving in that direction. As soon as she came near to where the woman stood relating her experience, she stepped forward, threw her arms around her neck, and burst into tears and said, "God bless you, my dear sister! God bless you!"

The woman responded with all her heart, and such a scene followed, so unpremeditated, so natural, so childlike, so overflowing with love that it melted the congregation to tears on every side. They wept on each other's necks. It was too moving a scene to be described in words.

The Baptist minister and I seldom met each other, though sometimes we were able to attend meetings together. He preached there half the time and I the other half; consequently I was generally away when he was there and he was generally absent when I was there. He was a good man and worked as best he could to promote the revival.

While I was laboring at this place the presbytery were called together to ordain me, which they did. Both churches were so strengthened and their numbers so greatly increased that they soon went forward and built each of them a commodious stone meeting house. I believe they have had a healthy state of religion there since that time.

The doctrines preached were those which I have always preached as the Gospel of Christ. I insisted upon the voluntary moral depravity of the unconverted, and the unalterable necessity of a radical change of heart by the Holy Spirit and by means of the truth.

I laid great stress upon prayer as an indispensable condition of promoting the revival. The atonement of Jesus Christ, his divinity, his divine mission, his perfect life, his vicarious death, his resurrection, and repentance, faith, justification by faith, and all the kindred doctrines were discussed as thoroughly as I was able, and pressed home, and were manifestly made effective by the power of the Holy Spirit.

The means used were simply preaching, prayer and conference meetings, much private prayer, much personal conversation, and meetings for the instruction of earnest inquirers. These, and no other means,

were used for the promotion of that work. There
was no appearance of fanaticism, no bad spirit, no
divisions, no heresies, no schisms. Neither at that time,
nor certainly so long as I was acquainted at that place,
was there any result of that revival to be lamented,
nor any feature of it that was of questionable effect.

I have spoken of cases of intensified opposition to
this revival. One circumstance, I found, had prepared
the people for this opposition and had greatly embit-
tered it. I found that region of country which, in the
western phrase, would be called "a burnt district."
A few years previously there had been a wild excitement passing through that region which they called
a revival but which turned out to be spurious. I can
give no account of it except what I heard from Christian
people and others. It was reported as having been a
very extravagant excitement, and resulted in a reaction
so extensive and profound as to leave the impression
on many minds that religion was a mere delusion.

I found that it had left among Christian people some
practices that were offensive, and calculated rather
to excite ridicule than any serious conviction of the
truth of religion. For example, in all their prayer meetings I found a custom prevailing like this: every professing Christian felt it a duty to testify for Christ.
They must "take up the cross" and say something in
the meeting. One would rise and say in substance: "I
have a duty to perform which no one can perform for
me. I arise to testify that religion is good; though I
must confess that I do not enjoy it at present. I have
nothing in particular to say, only to bear my testimony,
and I hope you will all pray for me."

This concluded, that person would sit down and another would rise and say, about to the same effect:
"Religion is good. I do not enjoy it and I have nothing
else to say, but I must do my duty. I hope you will
all pray for me." Thus the time would be occupied,

and the meeting would pass off with very little that was more interesting than such remarks as these. Of course the ungodly would make sport of this.

It was in fact ridiculous and repulsive. But the impression was rooted in the public mind that this was the way to hold a prayer and conference meeting, and that it was the duty of every professing Christian to give a testimony for God whenever an opportunity was afforded. I was obliged, for the purpose of getting rid of it, to hold no such meetings. Consequently, I appointed every meeting for preaching. When we were assembled I would begin by singing and then would pray myself. I would then call on one or two others to pray, naming them. Then I would name a text and talk for a while.

Then, when I saw that an impression was made, I would stop and ask one or two to pray that the Lord might fasten that on their minds. I would then proceed with my talk, and after a little, stop again and ask one or two to pray. Thus I would proceed without throwing the meeting open for remarks by the brothers and sisters. Then they would go away without being in bondage and not feeling that they had neglected their duty in not bearing testimony for God.

Thus most of our prayer meetings were not so in name. As they were appointed for preaching, it was not expected that they would be thrown open for everyone to speak. In this way I was able to overcome that silly method of holding meetings that created so much mirth and ridicule on the part of the ungodly.

After the revival took thorough hold in this place and those things occurred that I have named, opposition entirely ceased so far as I could learn. I spent more than six months at this place and at Antwerp, laboring between the two places. For the latter part of the time I heard nothing of open opposition.

During the whole six months that I labored in that

region I rode on horseback from town to town, and from settlement to settlement, in various directions, and preached the Gospel as I had opportunity. When I left Adams my health had run down a good deal. I had coughed blood, and at the time I was licensed my friends thought that I could live but a short time.

Mr. Gale charged me, when I left Adams, not to attempt to preach more than once a week, and then to be sure not to speak more than half an hour at a time. But instead of this I visited from house to house, attended prayer meetings, and preached and labored every day and almost every night through the whole season. Before the six months were completed my health was entirely restored, my lungs were sound, and I could preach two hours, or two hours and a half, or longer, without feeling the least fatigue. I think my sermons generally averaged nearly two hours. I preached outdoors; I preached in barns; I preached in schoolhouses; and a glorious revival spread all over that new region.

8

All through the earlier part of my ministry especially, I used to get a great many rebuffs and reproofs from ministers, particularly in respect to my manner of preaching. They would reprove me for illustrating my ideas by reference to the common affairs of men of different pursuits around me, as I was in the habit of doing. Among farmers and mechanics, and other classes of men, I borrowed my illustrations from their various occupations. I tried also to use language they would understand. I addressed them in the language of the common people. I sought to express all my ideas in few words, and in words that were in common use.

This was extremely contrary to the notions which at that time prevailed among ministers, and even yet prevail to a very great extent. In reference to my illustrations they would say, "Why don't you illustrate from events of ancient history, and take a more dignified way of illustrating your ideas?"

I defended myself by saying that my object was not to cultivate a style of oratory that should soar above the heads of the people, but to make myself understood; therefore I would use any language adapted to this end that did not involve coarseness or vulgarity.

They used to complain that I let down the dignity of the pulpit; that I was a disgrace to the ministerial profession; that I talked like a lawyer at the bar; that I talked to the people in a colloquial manner; that I said "you," instead of preaching about sin and sinners and saying "they"; that I said "hell," and with such emphasis I often shocked the people. Furthermore, they said that I urged the people with such vehemence, as if they might not have a moment to live; and sometimes they complained that I blamed the people too much.

After I had preached for some time and the Lord had everywhere added his blessing, whenever ministers contended with me about my manner of preaching and desired me to adopt their ideas and preach as they did, I used to say that I dared not make the changes they desired. I said, "Show me a more excellent way. Show me the fruits of your ministry, and if they so far exceed mine as to give me evidence that you have found a more excellent way, I will adopt your views."

They used to complain, oftentimes, that I was guilty of repetition in my preaching. I would take the same thought and turn it over and over, and illustrate it in various ways. I assured them that I thought it was necessary to do so to make myself understood, and that I could not be persuaded to relinquish this practice by any of their arguments.

Then they would say, "You will not interest the educated part of your congregation." But facts soon silenced them on this point. They found that under my preaching, judges, lawyers, and educated men were converted by the score; whereas, under their methods, such a thing seldom occurred.

In what I say upon this subject I hope my brethren will understand that I have only a kind and benevolent regard for their highest usefulness. I have always taken their criticisms kindly and given them credit for benevolent intentions. Now I am an old man, and many of the results of my views and methods are known to the public. Is it out of place for me to speak freely to the ministry upon this subject?

In reply to their objections I have sometimes told them what a judge of the Supreme Court remarked to me upon this subject. "Ministers," he said, "do not exercise good sense in addressing the people. They are afraid of repetition. They use language not well understood by the common people. Their illustrations are not taken from the common pursuits of life. They write in too elevated a style, read without repetition and are not understood by the people. Now," he continued, "if lawyers should take such a course, they would ruin themselves and their cause. When I was at the bar I used to take it for granted, when I had before me a jury of respectable men, that I should have to repeat over my main positions about as many times as there were persons in the jury box. I learned that unless I did so—illustrated, repeated, and turned over the main points of law and of evidence—I would lose my case. We are set on getting a verdict. Hence we are set upon being understood. We mean to convince them, to get a verdict, and to get it upon the spot; so that when they go to their room it will be found that they have understood us and that they have been convinced by the facts and arguments. Now, if ministers would do this, the effects of their preaching would be unspeakably different from what they are."

The more experience I had, the more I saw the results of my method of preaching. The more I conversed with all classes, high and low, educated and uneducated, the more I was confirmed that God had led me, had taught me, and had given me right conceptions in regard to the best manner of winning souls. I say that God taught me, and I know it must have been so, for surely I never had obtained these ideas from man. I mention this as a matter of duty, for I am still solemnly impressed with the conviction that the schools are to a great extent spoiling the ministers.

Ministers in these days have great facilities for obtaining information on all theological questions, and are vastly more learned, so far as theological, historical, and Bible learning is concerned, than they perhaps ever have been in any age of the world. Yet with all their learning they do not know how to use it. They are, after all, to a great extent like David in Saul's armor.

One great thing above all others that ministers need is singleness of purpose. If they have a reputation to secure and to nurse, they will do but little good. Many years ago a beloved pastor of my acquaintance left home for his health and employed a young man just out of seminary to fill his pulpit while he was absent. This young man wrote and preached as splendid sermons as he could.

The pastor's wife finally ventured to say to him, "You are preaching over the heads of our people. They do not understand your language or your illustrations. You bring too much of your learning into the pulpit."

He replied, "I am a young man. I am cultivating a style. I am aiming to prepare myself for occupying a pulpit and surrounding myself with a cultivated congregation. I cannot descend to your people. I must cultivate an elevated style."

A reflecting mind will feel as if it were infinitely out of place to present in the pulpit to immortal souls, hanging upon the verge of everlasting death, such specimens of learning and rhetoric. They know that men do not do so on any subject where they are really in earnest. The captain of a fire company, when a city is on fire, does not read to his company an essay or exhibit a fine specimen of rhetoric when he shouts to them and directs their movements. It is a question of urgency, and he intends that every word shall be understood. He is entirely in earnest with them, and they feel that criticism would be out of place in regard to the language he uses.

So it always is when men are entirely in earnest. Their language is in point, direct and simple. Their sentences are short, understandable, powerful. The appeal is made directly for action, and hence all such discourses take effect. This is the reason why, formerly, the ignorant Methodist preachers and the earnest Baptist preachers produced so much more effect than our most learned theologians and ministers. They do so now. The impassioned utterance of a common exhorter will often move a congregation far beyond anything that those splendid exhibitions of rhetoric can effect. Great sermons lead the people to praise the preacher. Good preaching leads the people to praise the Savior.

People have often said to me: "Why, you do not preach. You talk to the people."

A man in London went home from one of our meetings greatly convicted. He had been a skeptic. His wife, seeing him greatly excited, said to him, "Have you been to hear Mr. Finney preach?"

He replied: "I have been to Mr. Finney's meeting. He don't preach. He only explains what other people preach."

This, in substance, I have heard over and over again. "Why!" they say, "anybody could preach as you do. You just talk to the people. You talk as you would if you sat in the parlor."

Others have said: "Why, it don't seem like preaching, but it seems as if Mr. Finney had taken me alone and was talking with me face to face."

My habit has always been to study the Gospel and the best application of it, all the time. I do not confine myself to hours and days of writing my sermons, but my mind is always pondering the truths of the Gospel and the best ways of using them. I go among the people and learn their wants. Then, in the light of the Holy Spirit, I take a subject that I think will meet their present necessities. I think intensely on it and pray much over the subject on Sunday morning, for example, and get my mind full of it, and then go and pour it out to the people.

One great difficulty with a written sermon is that a man after he has prepared it needs to think but little of the subject. He needs to pray but little. He perhaps reads over his manuscript Saturday evening or Sunday morning, but he does not feel the necessity of being powerfully anointed, that his mouth may be opened and filled with arguments, and that he may be enabled to preach out of a full heart.

I am prepared to say, most solemnly, that I think I have studied all the more for not having written my sermons. I have been obliged to make the subjects upon which I preached familiar to my thoughts, to fill my mind with them, and then go and talk them off to the people. I simply note the main points on which I wish to swell in the briefest possible manner, and in a language not a word of which I use, perhaps, in preaching.

When I first began to preach I didn't even do this. For some twelve years of my earliest ministry I wrote not a word and was most commonly obliged to preach without any preparation whatever, except what I got in prayer. I depended on the occasion and the Holy Spirit to suggest the text and to open up the whole subject to my mind. If I did not preach from inspiration, I don't know how I did preach. It seemed that I could see with intuitive clearness just what I ought to say, and whole platoons of thoughts, words and illustrations came to me as fast as I could deliver them. When I first began to make outlines I made them after, and not before, I preached. It was to preserve the outline of the thought which had been given me. But after all, I have never found myself able to use old outlines in preaching without remodelling them and having a fresh and new view of the subject given me by the Holy Spirit.

I almost always get my subjects on my knees in prayer; and it has been a common experience with me, upon receiving a subject from the Holy Spirit, to have it make so strong an impression on my mind as to make me tremble, so that I could with difficulty write. When subjects are thus given me that seem to go through me, body and soul, I can in a few moments make out an outline that enables me to retain the view presented by the Spirit. I find that such sermons always tell with great power upon the people.

Let no man say that this is claiming a higher inspiration than is promised to ministers, or than ministers have a right to expect. For I believe that all ministers, called by Christ to preach the Gospel, ought to be, and may be, in such a sense inspired as to "preach the Gospel with the Holy Spirit sent down from heaven."

What else did Christ mean when he said, "Go and disciple all nations; and lo! I am with you always, even unto the end of the world"? What did he mean when he said, speaking of the Holy Spirit, "He shall take of mine and show it to you. He shall bring all things to your remembrance, whatsoever I have said unto you"? What did he mean when he said, "If any man believe in me, out of his heart shall flow rivers of living water"? "This spoke he of the Spirit, which they that believe on him should receive."

All ministers may be, and ought to be, so filled with the Holy Spirit that all who hear them shall be impressed with the conviction that "God is in them of a truth!"

9

I must now give some account of my labors and their result at Antwerp, a village north of Evans' Mills.

I arrived there the first time in April, and found that no religious services of any kind were held in the town. The land in the township belonged to a rich landholder residing in Ogdensburgh. To encourage the settlement of the township he had built a brick meeting house. But the people had no mind to keep up public worship and therefore the meeting house was locked up, and the key was in the possession of a Mr. C—— who kept the village hotel.

I found Mrs. C——, the landlady, a pious woman. There were two other pious women in the village, the wife of a merchant and the wife of a physician. It was on Friday, if I remember right, that I arrived there. I called on those pious women and asked them if they would like to have a meeting. They said they would but they did not know if it would be possible. The merchant's wife agreed to open her parlor that evening for a meeting if I could get anybody to attend.

I went about and invited the people and secured the attendance of some thirteen. I preached to them and then said that if I could get the use of the village schoolhouse, I would preach on Sunday. I got the consent of the trustees, and the next day a notice was circulated among the people for a meeting at the schoolhouse Sunday morning.

In passing around the village I heard a vast amount of profanity. I thought I had never heard so much in any place that I had ever visited. It seemed as if the men, in playing ball upon the green and in every business place that I stepped into, were all cursing and swearing and damning each other. I felt as if I had arrived upon the borders of hell. I had a kind of awful feeling as I passed around the village on Saturday. The very atmosphere seemed to me to be poison, and a kind of terror took possession of me.

I gave myself to prayer on Saturday and urged my petition until this answer came: "Be not afraid, but speak and hold not your peace; for I am with you, and no man shall set on you to hurt you. For I have many people in this city." This completely relieved me of all fear. I found, however, that the Christian people there were really afraid that something serious might happen if religious meetings were again established in that place. I spent Saturday very much in prayer, but passed around the village enough to see that the notice that had been given out for preaching in the schoolhouse was making quite an excitement.

Sunday morning I arose and left my lodgings in the hotel, and in order to get alone where I could let out my voice as well as my heart, I went up into the woods at some distance from the village and continued for a considerable time in prayer. However, I did not get relief and went up a second time, but the load upon my mind increased and I did not find relief. I went up a third time, and then the answer came. I found that it was time for the meeting and went immediately to the schoolhouse. I found it packed to its utmost capacity. I had my pocket Bible in my hand and read to them this text: "God so loved the world that he gave his only begotten son, that whosoever believes in him might not perish but have everlasting life." I cannot remember much what I said, but I know

that the point on which my mind principally labored
was the treatment which God received in return for
his love. The subject affected my own mind very much,
and I preached and poured out my soul and my tears
together.

I saw several of the men there from whom I had,
the day before, heard the most awful profanity. I pointed them out in the meeting and told what they said—
how they called on God to damn each other. Indeed,
I let loose my whole heart upon them. I told them
they seemed "to howl blasphemy about the streets like
hell-hounds," and it seemed to me as if I had arrived
"on the very edge of hell." Everybody knew that what
I said was true, and they quailed under it. They did
not appear offended, and the people wept about as much
as I did myself. I don't think there were any dry eyes
in the house.

Mr. C——, the landlord, had refused to open the
meeting house in the morning. But as soon as these
first services closed he arose and said to the people
that he would open the meeting house in the afternoon.

The people scattered and carried the information
in every direction, and in the afternoon the meeting
house was nearly as much crowded as the schoolhouse
had been in the morning. Everybody was out at the
meeting, and the Lord let me loose upon them in a
wonderful manner. My preaching seemed to them to
be something new. Indeed it seemed to myself as if
I could rain hail and love upon them at the same time;
or in other words, that I could rain upon them hail
in love. It seemed as if my love for God, in view of
the abuse which they heaped upon him, sharpened up
my mind to the most intense agony. I felt like rebuking
them with all my heart and yet with a compassion
which they could not mistake. I never knew that they
accused me of severity, although I think I never spoke
with more severity in my life.

The labors of this day were effectual, convicting the great mass of population. From that day wherever I appointed a meeting, the people would throng to hear. The work immediately began and went forward with great power. I preached twice in the village church on Sunday, attended a prayer meeting in the early afternoon and generally preached somewhere, in a schoolhouse in the neighborhood, at five o'clock in the afternoon.

On the third Sunday that I preached there an aged man came to me as I was entering the pulpit and asked me if I would go and preach in a schoolhouse in his neighborhood, about three miles distant, saying that they had never had any services there. He wished me to come as soon as I could. I appointed the next day, Monday, at five o'clock in the afternoon. It was a warm day. I left my horse at the village and thought I would walk down so that I should have no trouble along the way in calling on the people in the neighborhood of the schoolhouse. However, before I reached the place, having labored so hard on Sunday, I found myself very much exhausted and sat down by the way and felt as if I could scarcely proceed. I blamed myself for not having taken my horse.

But at the appointed hour I found the schoolhouse full, and I could only get a standing place near the open door. I read a hymn, but I cannot call it singing, for they seemed never to have had any church music in that place. However, the people pretended to sing. It sounded like each one was bawling in his own way. My ears had been cultivated by teaching church music, and their horrible discord distressed me so much that, at first, I thought I must go out. I finally put both hands over my ears and held them with my full strength. But this did not shut out the discords. I stood it, however, until they were through and then I cast myself down on my knees, almost in a state of desperation and began to pray. The Lord opened the windows of heaven, the spirit of prayer was poured out, and I let my whole heart out in prayer.

I had taken no thought with regard to a text upon which to preach, but waited to see the congregation. As soon as I was through praying, I arose from my knees and said: "Up, get you out of this place; for the Lord will destroy this city." I told them I did not remember exactly where that text was, but I told them very nearly where they would find it and then went on to explain it.

I told them about a man named Abraham and his nephew Lot; how they separated from each other on account of differences between their herdmen; and that Abraham took the hill country, and Lot settled in the vale of Sodom. I then told them how exceedingly wicked Sodom became, and what abominable practices they fell into. I told them that the Lord decided to destroy Sodom, and visited Abraham to inform him what he was about to do. Abraham prayed to the Lord to spare Sodom if he found a certain number of righteous people there, and the Lord promised to do so for their sakes. But it was found that there was only one righteous person there and that was Lot, Abraham's nephew.

While I was relating these facts I observed the people looking as if they were angry. Many of the men were in their shirt sleeves, and they looked at each other and at me as if they were ready to fall upon me and chastise me on the spot. I saw their strange and unaccountable looks, and could not understand what I was saying that had offended them. However, it seemed to me that their anger rose higher and higher as I continued the narrative. As soon as I had finished the story I said that I understood they had never had a religious meeting in that place; therefore I had a right to take it for granted, and was compelled to take it for granted, that they were ungodly people. I pressed that home to them with more and more energy, with my heart full almost to bursting.

I had not spoken to them in this strain of direct application more than a quarter of an hour when all at once an awful solemnity seemed to settle down upon them. The congregation began to fall from their seats in every direction and cry for mercy. If I had had a sword in each hand I could not have cut them off their seats as fast as they fell. Indeed, nearly the whole congregation were either on their knees or prostrate in less than two minutes from this first shock that fell upon them. Everyone who was able to speak at all prayed for himself.

Of course I was obliged to stop preaching, for they no longer paid any attention. I saw the old man who had invited me there to preach, sitting about in the middle of the house and looking around with utter amazement. I raised my voice almost to a scream to make him hear above the noise of the sobbing, and pointing to him said, "Can't you pray?"

He instantly fell upon his knees, and with a stentorian voice poured himself out to God, but he did not at all get the attention of the people.

I then spoke as loudly as I could, and tried to make them listen to me. I said to them, "You are not in hell yet. Now let me direct you to Christ."

For a few moments I tried to hold forth the Gospel to them, but scarcely any of them paid any attention. My heart was so overflowing with joy at such a scene that I could hardly contain myself. It was with much difficulty that I refrained from shouting and giving glory to God.

As soon as I could sufficiently control my feelings I turned to a young man who was close to me, and was engaged in praying for himself, laid my hand on his shoulder, thus getting his attention, and preached Jesus in his ear. As soon as I got his attention to the cross of Christ, he believed, was calm and quiet for a minute or two, and then broke out in praying for the others. I then turned to another, and took the same course with him, with the same result, and then another, and another.

In this way I kept on until I found the time had arrived when I must leave them and go to fulfill an appointment in the village. I told them this, and asked the old man who had invited me there to remain and take charge of the meeting while I went to my appointment. He did so. But there was too much interest, and there were too many wounded souls, to dismiss the meeting; and so it was held all night. In the morning there were still those there that could not get away, and they carried on in a private house in the neighborhood, to make room for the school. In the afternoon they sent for me to come down there, as they could not yet break up the meeting.

When I went down the second time, I was told why the congregation manifested such anger during the introduction of my sermon the day before. I learned that the place was called Sodom, but I hadn't known it; and that there was but one pious man in the place and his name was Lot! This was the old man who invited me there. The people supposed that I had chosen my subject and preached to them in that manner because they were so wicked as to be called Sodom. This was a striking coincidence, but so far as I was concerned it was altogether accidental.

10

There was a Presbyterian church in Antwerp consisting of a few members. Some years before they had tried to keep up a meeting at the village on Sundays. But one of the elders who conducted their Sunday meetings lived about five miles out of the village, and was obliged, in approaching the village, to pass through a Universalist settlement. The Universalists had broken up the village meeting by making it impossible for Deacon R——, as they called him, to get through their settlement to the meetings. They would even take off the wheels of his carriage. When the revival in Antwerp got its full strength, Deacon R—— wanted me to go and preach in that neighborhood. Accordingly I made an appointment to preach on a certain afternoon in their schoolhouse. When I arrived I found the schoolhouse filled, and Deacon R—— sitting near a window by a stand with a Bible and hymn book on it. I sat down beside him, then arose and read a hymn, and they sang after a fashion. I then engaged in prayer, and had great access to the throne of grace. After prayer I arose and read this text: "You serpents, you generation of vipers, how can you escape the damnation of hell?"

I saw that Deacon R—— was very uneasy, and he soon got up and went to stand in the open door. There were some boys near the door and I supposed at the time that he had gone to keep the boys still. But afterward I learned that it was through fear. He thought that if they set upon me, he would be where he could escape. From my text he concluded that I was going to deal very plainly with them. He had been quite nervous by the opposition they had given him, and wanted to keep out of their reach. I proceeded to pour myself out upon them with all my might, and before I was through, there was a complete upturning of the very foundations of Universalism in that place. The scene almost equalled that of which I have spoken in Sodom. Thus the revival penetrated to every part of the town, and some of the neighboring towns shared in the blessing. The work was very precious in this place.

When we came to receive the converts, after a great number had been examined and the day approached for their admission, I found that several of them had been brought up in Baptist families. I asked them if they would not prefer to be immersed. They said they had no preference, but their parents would prefer to have them immersed. I told them I had no objection to immersing them if they thought it would please their friends better and themselves as well. Accordingly, when Sunday came I arranged to baptize by immersion during the afternoon. We went down to a stream that runs through the place, and there I baptized about a dozen or more.

When the hour for late afternoon services arrived we went to the meeting house, and there I baptized a great number of persons by taking water in my hand and applying it to the forehead. The administration of the ordinance in the church was so manifestly owned and blessed of God as to do much to satisfy the people that that mode of baptism also was acceptable to him.

There were a great many interesting cases of conversion in this place as well as two very striking cases of instantaneous recovery from insanity during this revival. As I went into the meeting in the afternoon one Sunday, I saw several ladies sitting in a pew, with a woman dressed in black who seemed to be in great distress of mind. They were partly holding her, preventing her from going out. As I came in, one of the ladies came to me and told me that she was an insane woman. She had been a Methodist, but had, as she supposed, fallen from grace, which had led to despair and finally to insanity. Her husband was an intemperate man and lived several miles from the village. He had brought her down and left her at the meeting and had himself gone to the tavern. I said a few words to her, but she replied that she must leave. She could not bear to hear any praying, or preaching, or singing. Hell was her portion, and she could not endure anything that made her think of heaven.

I cautioned the ladies, privately, to keep her in her seat if they could, without disturbing the meeting. I then went into the pulpit and read a hymn. As soon as the singing began she struggled hard to get out. But the ladies obstructed her passage, and kindly but persistently prevented her escape. After a few moments she became quiet, but seemed to avoid hearing or attending at all to the singing. I then prayed. For some little time I heard her struggling to get out, but before I had finished she became quiet and the congregation was still. The Lord gave me a great spirit of prayer, and a text, for I had no text settled upon before. I took my text from Hebrews: "Let us come boldly unto the throne of grace, that we may obtain mercy and find grace to help in time of need."

My object was to encourage faith in ourselves and in her, and in ourselves for her. When I began to pray, she at first made quite an effort to get out. The ladies kindly resisted, and she finally sat still but held her head very low, and seemed determined not to listen to what I said. But as I proceeded she began gradually to raise her head and to look at me from within her long black bonnet. She looked up more and more until she sat upright and looked me in the face with intense earnestness. As I proceeded to urge the people to be bold in their faith, to launch out and commit themselves with the utmost confidence to God through the atoning sacrifice of our great High Priest, all at once she startled the congregation by uttering a loud shriek. She then almost cast herself from her seat and held her head very low. I could see that she "trembled very exceedingly." The ladies in the pew with her partly supported her and watched her with manifest prayerful interest and sympathy. As I proceeded she began to look up again and soon sat upright, with her face wonderfully changed, indicating triumphant joy and peace. There was such a glow upon her countenance as I have seldom seen in any human face. Her joy was so great that she could scarcely contain herself until the meeting was over, and then she soon made everybody around her understand that she was set at liberty. About two years later I met her and found her still full of joy and peace.

The other case of recovery was that of a woman who had also fallen into despair and insanity. I was not present when she was restored, but was told that it was almost instantaneous, by means of a baptism of the Holy Spirit. Revivals are sometimes accused of making people mad. The fact is, men are naturally mad on the subject of religion, and revivals restore them rather than make them mad.

During this revival we heard much of opposition to it from Gouverneur, a town about twelve miles farther north. We heard that the wicked threatened to come down and mob us and break up our meetings. Of course we paid no attention to that.

At this time I was earnestly pressed to remain at Evans' Mills, and finally gave them encouragement that I would stay with them at least one year. Being engaged to marry, I went from there to Whitestown, Oneida County, and was married in October, 1824. My wife had made preparations for housekeeping, and a day or two after our marriage I left her and returned to Evans' Mills to obtain conveyance to transport our goods to that place. I told her that she might expect me back in about a week.

The fall previous to this I had preached a few times in the evening in a place called Perch River, still farther northwest from Evans' Mills, about twelve miles. I spent one Sunday at Evans' Mills, and intended to return for my wife about the middle of that week. But a messenger from Perch River came up that Sunday and said there had been a revival working its way slowly among the people ever since I preached there, and he begged me to go down and preach at least once more. I sent word that I would be there Tuesday night. But I found the interest so deep that I stayed and preached Wednesday and Thursday night. I then felt that I could not return for my wife but must continue to preach in that neighborhood.

The revival soon spread in the direction of Brownville, a considerable village several miles southwest of that place. Finally, under the pressing invitation of the minister and church at Brownville, I spent the winter, having written to my wife that such were the circumstances that I must defer coming for her until God seemed to open the way.

At Brownville there was a very interesting work. But still the church was in such a state that it was very difficult to get them into the work. I could not find much that seemed to me to be sound-hearted piety, and the policy of the minister was really such as to forbid anything like a general sweep of revival. I labored there that winter with great pain and had many serious obstacles to overcome. Sometimes I would find

that the minister and his wife were away from our meetings, and would learn afterward that they had stayed
away to attend a party.

I was the guest of a Mr. B——, one of the elders
of the church and the most intimate and influential
friend of the minister. One day as I came down from
my room and was going out to call on some inquirers,
I met Mr. B—— in the hall. He said to me, "Mr. Finney,
what would you think of a man who was praying week
after week for the Holy Spirit and could get no answer?"

I replied that I would think he was praying from
false motives.

"But from what motives," said he, "should a man
pray? If he wants to be happy, is that a false motive?"

I replied, "Satan might pray with as good a motive
as that," and then quoted the words of the Psalmist:
" 'Uphold me with thy free spirit. Then will I teach
transgressors thy ways, and sinners shall be converted
unto thee.' See?" I said, "the Psalmist did not pray
for the Holy Spirit that he might be happy, but that
he might be useful and that sinners might be converted
to Christ." I said this, turned and went out immediately, and he turned abruptly and went back to his room.

I remained out until dinner time, and when I returned he met me and immediately began to confess.
"Mr. Finney," he said, "I owe you a confession. I was
angry when you said that to me, and I must confess
that I hoped I would never see you again. What you
said," he continued, "forced the conviction upon me
that I never had been converted, that I never had had
any higher motive than a mere selfish desire for my
own happiness. I went away after you left the house
and prayed to God to take my life. I could not endure
to have it known that I had always been deceived. I
have been most intimate with our minister. I have
journeyed with him and slept with him and conversed

with him, and have been more intimate with him than any other member of the church, and yet I saw that I had always been a deceived hypocrite. The mortification was intolerable," he said, "and I wanted to die, and prayed the Lord to take my life." However, he was all broken down then, and from that time became a new man.

That conversion did a great deal of good. I might relate many other interesting facts connected with this revival, but as there were so many things that pained me in regard to the relation of the pastor to it, and especially of the pastor's wife, I will forbear.

Early in the spring, 1825, I left Brownville with my horse and cutter to go after my wife. I had been absent six months since our marriage; and as mails then were between us, we had seldom been able to exchange letters. I drove on some fifteen miles. The roads were very slippery. My horse was smooth shod, and I realized that I must have his shoes reset. I stopped at LeRayville, a small village about three miles south of Evans' Mills. While my horse was being shod, the people, finding that I was there, ran to me and wanted to know if I would not preach at one o'clock in the schoolhouse, for they had no meeting house.

At one o'clock the house was packed, and while I preached the Spirit of God came down with great power upon the people. So great and evident was the outpouring of the Spirit that in compliance with their earnest entreaty, I decided to spend the night there and preach again in the evening. But the work increased more and more. In the evening I appointed another meeting in the morning, and in the morning I appointed another in the evening, and soon I saw that I would not be able to go any farther after my wife. I told a brother that if he would take my horse and cutter and go after my wife, I would remain. He did so, and I went on preaching from day to day, and from night to night, and there was a powerful revival.

After laboring there a few weeks, the great mass of the inhabitants were converted. Among the others was Judge C——, a man of influence, standing head and shoulders above all the people around him. My wife arrived a few days after I sent for her, and we accepted the invitation of Judge C—— and his wife to become their guests.

11

While I was at Brownville God revealed to me, all at once in a most unexpected manner, the fact that he was going to pour out his Spirit at Gouverneur, and that I must go there and preach. Of the place I knew absolutely nothing except that in that town there had been so much opposition to the revival in Antwerp the year before. I can never tell how or why the Spirit of God made that revelation to me. But I knew then, and I have no doubt now, that it was a direct revelation from God to me. I had not thought of the place for months, but in prayer it was shown to me as clear as light that I must go and preach in Gouverneur and that God would pour out his Spirit there.

Very soon after this I saw one of the members of the church from Gouverneur who was passing through Brownville. I told him what God had revealed to me. He stared at me as if he supposed I was insane. But I charged him to go home and tell the others what I said so that they might prepare themselves for my coming and for the outpouring of the Lord's Spirit.

I had to ride nearly thirty miles to reach the place. In the morning it rained very hard, but the rain let up in time for me to ride to Antwerp. While I was getting dinner at that place the rain came on again and literally poured until quite late in the afternoon. However, the rain let up again in time for me to ride rapidly to Gouverneur. I found that the people had given up expecting me that day because of the great rain.

Before I reached the village I met one of the principal members of the church returning from the church meeting to his house, which I had just passed. He stopped his carriage and addressing me said, "Is this Mr. Finney?"

After my reply in the affirmative he said, "Please go back to my house, for I shall insist on your being my guest. You are fatigued with the long ride and the roads are so bad, you will not have any meeting tonight."

I replied that I must fulfill my appointment and asked him if the church meeting had adjourned. He said it had not when he left, and he thought it possible I might reach the village before they would dismiss.

I rode rapidly on, alighted at the meeting house door and hurried in. Brother Nash had gone to Gouverneur earlier to prepare the people for my coming, and was standing in front of the pulpit, having just risen to dismiss the meeting. On seeing me enter, he held up his hands and waited until I came near the pulpit and then he took me right in his arms. After thus embracing me he introduced me to the congregation. I informed them that I had come to fulfill my appointment, and, the Lord willing, I would preach at a certain hour which I named.

When the hour arrived, the house was filled. The people had heard enough, for and against me, to have their curiosity excited, and there was a general turning out. The Lord gave me a text and I went into the pulpit and let my heart out to the people. The word took powerful effect. That was evident to everybody. I dismissed the meeting and that night got some rest.

There were two churches in the town standing near each other, a Baptist church and a Presbyterian. The Baptist church had a pastor but the Presbyterian had none. As soon as the revival broke out and attracted general attention the Baptist brethren began to oppose it. They spoke against it and used very objectionable means indeed to arrest its progress. This encouraged a set of young men to join hand in hand to strengthen each other in opposition to the work. The Baptist church was quite influential, and the stand they took greatly emboldened the opposition and seemed to give it a peculiar bitterness and strength, as might be expected. Those young men seemed to stand like a bulwark in the way of the progress of the work.

In this state of things brother Nash and I, after consultation, made up our minds that the situation must be overcome by prayer, and that it could not be reached in any other way. We therefore retired to a grove and gave ourselves to prayer until we prevailed and felt confident that no power on earth or hell could stop the revival.

The next Sunday, after I had preached morning and afternoon—for I did all the preaching and brother Nash gave himself continually to prayer—we met at five o'clock in the church for a prayer meeting. The meeting house was filled. Near the close of the meeting brother Nash arose and addressed that company of young men who had joined hand in hand to resist the revival. I believe they were all there, and they sat braced up against the Spirit of God. What they heard and saw was too solemn for them to ridicule, and yet their brazen-facedness and stiff-neckedness were apparent to everybody.

Brother Nash addressed them very earnestly and pointed out the guilt and danger of the course they were taking. Toward the close of his address he waxed exceedingly warm and said to them, "Now mark me, young men! God will break your ranks in less than one week, either by converting some of you or by sending some of you to hell. He will do this as certainly

as the Lord is my God!" He was standing in front
of a pew, and when he brought his hand down it hit
the top of the pew before him so hard that it made
it thoroughly jar. He sat down immediately, dropped
his head and groaned with pain.

The house was as still as death, and most of the
people held down their heads. I could see that the young
men were agitated. For myself, I regretted that brother
Nash had gone so far. He had committed himself that
God would either take the life of some of them and
send them to hell, or convert some of them within a
week.

On Tuesday morning of the same week the leader
of these young men came to me in great distress of
mind. He was all prepared to submit, and as soon as
I came to press him he broke down like a child, confessed, and gave himself to Christ. Then he said, "What
shall I do, Mr. Finney?"

I replied, "Go immediately to all your young companions and pray with them and exhort them at once
to turn to the Lord." He did so, and before the week
was out all of those young men were trusting in Christ.

After the conversion of that class of young men,
as well as a number of others, I thought it was time,
if possible, to put a stop to the opposition of the Baptist
church and minister. I therefore had an interview first
with a deacon of the Baptist church, who had been
very bitter in his opposition, and said to him, "Now
you have carried your opposition far enough. You must
be satisfied that this is the work of God. I have made
no mention in public of your opposition, and I do not
wish to do so, or to appear to know that there is any
such thing, but you have gone far enough. I shall feel
it my duty, if you do not stop immediately, to take
you in hand and expose your opposition from the pulpit." Things had got into such a state that I was sure
that both God and the public would sustain me in car-

rying out the measure that I proposed.

He confessed and said that he was sorry, and promised that he would make confession and that he would not oppose the work any more. He said that he had made a great mistake and had been deceived, but that he also had been very wicked about it. He then went after his minister and I had a long conversation with them together. The minister confessed that he had been all wrong, that he had been deceived and had been wicked, and that his sectarian feeling had carried him too far. He hoped that I would forgive him, and prayed God to forgive him. I told him that I would take no notice whatever of the opposition of his church provided they stopped it, which they promised to do.

But I then said to him, "Now a considerable number of the young people, whose parents belong to your church, have been converted." As many as forty of their young people had been converted in that revival. "Now," I said, "if you go to proselytizing, that will create a sectarian feeling in both churches and will be worse than any opposition which you have offered." I said to him, "In spite of your opposition the work has gone on, because the Presbyterian brethren have kept clear of a sectarian spirit and have had the spirit of prayer. But if you go to proselytizing, it will destroy the spirit of prayer and will stop the revival immediately."

He knew it, he said, and therefore he would say nothing about receiving any of the converts, and would not open the doors of the church for their reception until the revival was over; and then, without any proselytizing, let the converts all join whichever church they pleased.

This was on Friday. The next day, Saturday, was the day for their monthly covenant meeting. When they had gathered, instead of keeping his word, he threw the doors of the church open and invited the converts to come forward and tell their experience and join the church. As many as could be persuaded to do so told their experience, and the next day there was a great parade of baptizing them. The minister sent off immediately and secured the help of one of the most proselytizing Baptist ministers that I ever knew. He came in and began to preach and lecture on baptism.

They traversed the town for converts in every direction, and whenever they could find anyone to join, they would get up a procession, march, sing, and make a great parade in going to the water to baptize them by immersion. This soon so grieved the Presbyterian church as to destroy their spirit of prayer and faith, and the work came to a dead stand. For six weeks there was not a single conversion. All, both saints and sinners, were discussing the question of baptism.

I finally said to the people one Sunday, "You see how it is, that the work of conversion is suspended, and we do not know that a conversion has occurred now for six weeks, and you know the reason." I did not tell them at all how the pastor of the Baptist church had violated his word, nor did I hint at it, for I knew that it would do no good, only much hurt, to inform the people that he had been guilty of taking such a course. But I said to them, "Now I do not want to take up a Sunday in preaching on this subject, but if you will come on Wednesday afternoon at one o'clock and bring your Bibles and your pencils to mark the passages, I will read to you all the passages in the Bible that relate to the mode of baptism. I will give you, as nearly as I understand them, the views of our Baptist brethren on all those passages, together with my own, and you shall judge for yourselves where the truth lies."

When Wednesday came the house was crowded. I saw quite a number of the Baptist brethren present. I began and read, first in the Old Testament and then in the New, all the passages that had any reference to the mode of baptism, so far as I knew. I gave the views that the Baptists had of those texts and the reasons for their views. I then gave my own views and my reasons for them. I saw that the impression was decided and good, and that no bad spirit prevailed, and the people appeared satisfied in regard to the manner of baptism. The Baptist brethren were quite satisfied that I stated their views fairly, and as strongly as they could state them themselves, and also their reasons for them. Before I dismissed the meeting I said, "If you will come tomorrow, at the same hour, one o'clock, I will read to you all the passages in the Bible that relate to the subjects eligible for baptism, and pursue the same course as I have done today."

The next day the house was crowded, if possible with more than the day before. Quite a number of the principal Baptist brethren were present, and I observed the old deacon, the great proselyter, sitting in the congregation. After going through the introductory services I arose and began my reading.

At this point the Baptist deacon arose and said, "Mr. Finney, I have an appointment and cannot stay to hear your readings. But I shall wish to answer you. How shall I know what course you take?"

I replied to him, "I have before me a little outline, wherein I quote all the passages that I shall read, and note the order in which I discuss the subject. You can have these notes, if you wish, and reply to it." He then went out, and, as I supposed, went away to attend his appointment.

I then took up the covenant made with Abraham, and read everything in the Old Testament that directly bore upon the question of the relation of families and of children to that covenant. I gave the Baptist view of the passages that I read, together with my own, with the reasons on both sides, as I had done the day before. I then took up the New Testament and went through with all the passages in that, referring to the subject. The people became very mellow, and the tears flowed very freely when I held up that covenant as still the covenant which God makes with parents and their household. The congregation was much moved and melted.

Just before I was through, the deacon of the Presbyterian church had occasion to go out with a child that had sat with him during the long meeting. He told me afterward, that as he went into the entrance hall of the church, he found the old Baptist deacon sitting there with the door ajar, listening to what I was saying and absolutely weeping himself.

When I was done the people thronged around me on every side and with tears thanked me for so full and satisfactory an exhibition of that subject. The meeting had been attended not only by members of the church but also by the community generally. The question was intelligently settled and soon the people ceased to talk about it. In the course of a few days the spirit of prayer returned, and the revival was revived and went on again with great power.

12

From Gouverneur I went to DeKalb, another village still farther north some sixteen miles. Here were a Presbyterian church and minister, but the church was small and the minister did not seem to have a very strong hold upon the people. However, I think he was decidedly a good man. I began to hold meetings in different parts of the town.

A few years previously there had been a revival in DeKalb under the labors of the Methodists. It had been attended with a good deal of excitement, and many cases had occurred of what the Methodists call "falling under the power of God." This the Presbyterians had resisted; consequently a bad state of feeling had arisen between the Methodists and the Presbyterians. The Methodists accused the Presbyterians of having opposed the revival among them because of these cases of falling. As nearly as I could learn, there was a good deal of truth in this, and the Presbyterians had been decidedly in error.

I had not preached very long one evening when just at the close of my sermon, I observed a man fall from his seat near the door, and the people gathered around him to take care of him. From what I saw I was satisfied that it was a case of falling under the power of God, as the Methodists would express it, and supposed that it was a Methodist. I must say I had a little fear that it might reproduce that state of division and alienation which had existed before. But on inquiry I learned that it was one of the principal members of the Presbyterian church that had fallen! And it was remarkable that during this revival there were several cases of this kind among the Presbyterians but none among the Methodists. This led to such confessions and explanations among the members of the different churches as to secure a state of great cordiality and good feeling among them.

While laboring at DeKalb I first became acquainted with Mr. F—— of Ogdensburgh. He heard of the revival in DeKalb and came some sixteen miles from Ogdensburgh to see it. He was wealthy and benevolent. He proposed to employ me as his missionary to work in the towns through that county, and he would pay me a salary. However, I declined to pledge myself to preach in any particular place or to confine my labors within any given lines.

Mr. F—— spent several days with me, visiting from house to house and attending our meetings. He had been educated in Philadelphia, an old school Presbyterian, and was himself an elder in the Presbyterian church in Ogdensburgh. When he departed he left a letter for me containing three ten dollar bills. A few days later he came up again and spent two or three days, attended our meetings and became very much interested in the work. When he went away he left another letter, containing, as before, three ten dollar bills. Thus I found myself possessed of sixty dollars, with which I immediately purchased a carriage. Before this time I had no carriage, though I had a horse, so my young wife and I used to go a good deal on foot to the meetings.

One Saturday, just before evening, a German merchant tailor from Ogdensburgh called on me and informed me that Squire F—— had sent him from Ogdens-

burgh to take my measurements for a suit. I had begun
to need clothes and had once, not long before, spoken
to the Lord about my clothes getting shabby, but it
had not occurred to me again. Mr. F——, however,
had observed it and sent this man, who was a Roman
Catholic, to take my measurements. I asked him if
he could stay over Sunday and take my measurements
Monday morning. I said, "It is too late for you to return
tonight, and if I allow you to take my measurements
tonight, you will go home tomorrow."

He admitted that he expected to do so. I said, "Then
you shall not take it. If you will not stay until Monday
morning, I will not be measured for a suit of clothes."
He remained.

A man named Elder S—— attended the meeting Sunday morning and at noon was invited by Elder B——
to go home with him and get some refreshment. Elder
B—— was full of the Holy Spirit and on the way home
he preached to Elder S——, who was at the time very
cold and backward in religion. Elder S—— was very
much penetrated by his words.

Soon after they entered the house the table was
spread, and they were invited to sit down and take
some refreshment. As they drew around the table Elder
S—— said to Elder B——, "How did you get this blessing?"

Elder B—— replied, "I stopped lying to God. All
my Christian life I have been making pretenses, and
asking God for things that I was not, on the whole,
willing to have. I had gone on and prayed as other
people prayed, and often had been insincere and really
lied to God. As soon as I made up my mind that I
never would say anything to God in prayer that I did
not really mean, God answered me, and the Spirit came
down and I was filled with the Holy Spirit."

At this moment Mr. S——, who had not begun to
eat, shoved his chair back from the table and fell on

his knees and began to confess how he had lied to God, and how he had played the hypocrite in his prayers as well as in his life. The Holy Spirit fell upon him immediately and filled him as full as he could hold.

In the afternoon the people assembled for worship and I stood in the pulpit reading a hymn. Soon two men came in. Elder E—— I knew, but Elder S—— was a stranger to me at that time. As soon as he came in the door he lifted his eyes to me, came straight up to the pulpit and took me up in his arms: "God bless you!" he said, "God bless you!" He then told me and the congregation what the Lord had just done for his soul.

His face was all aglow, and he was so changed in appearance that those who knew him were perfectly astonished at the change. When his son, who had not known of this change in his father, saw and heard him, he rose up and hurried out of the church. His father cried out, "Do not leave, my son, for I never loved you before!" He went on to speak, and the power with which he spoke was perfectly astonishing. The people melted down on every side, and his son broke down almost immediately.

Very soon the Roman Catholic tailor rose up and said, "I must tell you what the Lord has done for my soul. I was brought up a Roman Catholic, and I never dared to read my Bible. I was told that if I did, the devil would carry me off bodily. Sometimes when I dared look into it, it seemed as if the devil was peering over my shoulder and had come to carry me off. But," he said, "I see it is all a delusion." And he went on to tell what the Lord had done for him just there on the spot, what views the Lord had given him of the way of salvation by Jesus Christ. It was evident to everybody that he was converted.

This made a great impression on the congregation. I could not preach. The whole course of the meeting had taken on a type which the Lord had given it. I sat still and saw the salvation of God. All that afternoon conversions were multiplied in every part of the congregation. As they arose one after another and told what the Lord had done and was doing for their souls, the impression increased. So spontaneous a movement by the Holy Spirit, in convicting and converting sinners, I had scarcely ever seen.

In reflecting upon what I have said of these revivals in Jefferson and St. Lawrence counties, I am not quite sure that I have laid as much stress as I intended upon the agency of the Holy Spirit in those revivals.

I have said more than once that the spirit of prayer that prevailed in those revivals was a very marked feature of them. It was common for young converts to be greatly exercised in prayer. In some instances they were so burdened that they were constrained to pray whole nights, until their bodily strength was quite exhausted for the conversion of souls around them. There was a great pressure of the Holy Spirit upon the minds of Christians and they seemed to bear about with them the burden of immortal souls.

Not only were prayer meetings greatly multiplied and fully attended, not only was there great reverence in those meetings, but there was a mighty spirit of secret prayer. Christians prayed a great deal, many of them spending several hours in private prayer. In some instances two or more would take the promise, "If two of you shall agree on earth as touching anything that they shall ask, it shall be done for them of my Father which is in heaven," and make some particular person a subject of prayer. It was wonderful to what an extent they prevailed. Answers to prayer were so abundantly multiplied on every side that no one could escape the conviction that God was daily and hourly answering prayer.

If anything occurred that threatened to mar the

work, if there was any appearance of any root of bitterness springing up, or any tendency to fanaticism or disorder, Christians would take the alarm and give themselves to prayer that God would direct and control all things. It was surprising to see to what extent and by what means God would remove obstacles out of the way in answer to prayer.

In regard to my own experience, I will say that unless I had the spirit of prayer I could do nothing. If I lost the spirit of grace and supplication even for a day or an hour I found myself unable to preach with power and efficiency, or to win souls by personal conversation.

For several weeks before I left De Kalb I was strongly exercised in prayer and had an experience that was somewhat new to me. I found myself so much exercised, and so borne down with the weight of immortal souls, that I was constrained to pray without ceasing. Some of my experiences, indeed, alarmed me. A spirit of importunity sometimes came upon me so that I would say to God that he had made a promise to answer prayer, and I could not, and would not, be denied. I felt so certain that he would hear me, and that faithfulness to his promises and to himself made it impossible that he should not hear and answer, that frequently I found myself saying to him, "I hope thou dost not think that I can be denied. I come with thy faithful promises in my hand, and I cannot be denied." I cannot tell how absured unbelief looked to me, and how certain it was, in my mind, that God would answer the prayers which, from day to day, and from hour to hour, I found myself offering in such agony and faith. I had no idea what shape the answer would take, the locality in which the prayers would be answered, or the exact time of the answer. My impression was that the answer was near, even at the door, and I felt myself strengthened in the divine life. I put on the harness for a mighty conflict with the powers of darkness, and expected soon to see a far more powerful outpouring of the Spirit of God in that new country where I had been laboring.

13

In the early part of October the synod to which I belonged met in Utica. I took my wife and we went to Utica to attend the synod and to visit her father's family living near Utica.

Mr. Gale, my theological teacher, had left Adams not long after I left it myself, and had moved to a farm in the town of Western, Oneida County. Here he was endeavoring to regain his health, and was employed in teaching some young men who proposed to prepare themselves to preach the Gospel. I spent a few days at the synod at Utica and then set out on my return to my former field of labor.

We had not gone more than a dozen miles when we met Mr. Gale in his carriage, on his way to Utica. He leaped from his carriage and said, "God bless you, brother Finney! I was going down to the synod to see you. You must go home with me. I cannot be denied. I do not believe that I ever was converted, and I wrote the other day to Adams to find where a letter would reach you. I wanted to open my mind to you on the subject." He was so importunate that I consented, and we drove immediately to Western.

At this place began what was later called "The Western Revivals." These revivals are the ones that first attracted notice and excited the opposition of certain prominent ministers in the East and raised the cry of "New Measures."

I went directly to Mr. Gale's house and for several weeks was his guest. We arrived there Thursday, and that afternoon there was a scheduled prayer meeting in the schoolhouse near the church. The church had no regular minister and Mr. Gale was unable to preach because of poor health. There were three elders in the church and a few members, but the church was very small and religion was at low water mark. There seemed to be no life, or courage, or enterprise on the part of Christians. Nothing was being done to secure the conversion of sinners or the sanctification of the church members.

In the afternoon Mr. Gale invited me to go to the prayer meeting, and I went. They asked me to lead the meeting, but I declined, preferring rather to hear them pray and talk than to take part in the meeting myself. The meeting was opened by one of the elders, who read a chapter in the Bible and then a hymn, which they sang. After this he made a long prayer, or perhaps I should say an exhortation, or gave a narrative. I hardly know what to call it. He told the Lord how many years they had been holding that prayer meeting weekly, and that no answer had been given to their prayers. His statements and confessions greatly shocked me.

After he had ended, another elder took up the same theme. He read a hymn and, after singing, engaged in a long prayer in which he went over very nearly the same ground, making such statements as the first one had omitted.

Then followed the third elder in the same way. By this time I could say with Paul that my spirit was stirred within me. They had finished and were about to dismiss the meeting when one of the elders asked me if I would make a remark before they dismissed. I arose and took their statements and confessions for a text, and God inspired me to give them a terrible searching.

When I arose I had no idea what I should say, but the Spirit of God came upon me and I took up their prayers, statements and confessions and dissected them. I showed them up, and asked if it had been understood that that prayer meeting was a mock prayer meeting—whether they had come together just to mock God by implying that all the blame of what had been passing all this time was to be ascribed to his sovereighnty?

At first they all looked angry. Some of them afterward said that they were on the point of getting up and going out. But I followed them up on the track of their prayers and confessions until the elder, who was the principal man among them, who had opened the meeting, bursting into tears exclaimed, "Brother Finney, it is all true!" He fell upon his knees and wept aloud.

This was the signal for a general breaking. Every man and woman went down upon their knees. There were probably not more than a dozen present, but they were the leading members in the church. They all wept, confessed, and broke their hearts before God. This scene continued for an hour, and a more thorough breaking and confession I have seldom witnessed.

As soon as they recovered themselves somewhat they begged me to remain and preach to them on Sunday. I regarded it as the voice of the Lord and consented to do so. This was Thursday night. On Friday my mind was greatly exercised. I went off frequently into the church to engage in secret prayer, and had a mighty hold upon God. The news was circulated, and on Sunday the church was full of hearers. I preached all day and God came down with great power upon the people. It was evident to everybody that the work of grace had begun. I made appointments to preach in different parts of the town, in schoolhouses and at the center during the week, and the work increased from day to day.

In the meantime, my own mind was much exercised in prayer, and I found that the spirit of prayer was prevailing, especially among the women members of the church. The wives of two of the elders of the church were almost immediately greatly exercised in prayer. Each of them had families of unconverted children, and they laid hold in prayer with an earnestness that, to me, gave promise that their families must be converted. One of these women was in very feeble health and had not ventured out much to any meeting for a long time. But as the day was pleasant, she was out at the prayer meeting to which I have referred, and seemed to catch the inspiration of that meeting and took it home with her.

It was the next week that I called at this elder's home and found him pale and agitated. He said to me, "Brother Finney, I think my wife will die. She is so exercised in her mind that she cannot rest day or night, but is given up entirely to prayer, and I am afraid it will overcome her strength."

Hearing my voice in the sitting room she came out of her bedroom. Upon her face was a most heavenly glow. Her countenance was lighted up with a hope and a joy that were plainly from heaven. She exclaimed, "Brother Finney, the Lord has come! This work will spread over all this region! A cloud of mercy overhangs us all, and we shall see such a work of grace as we have never yet seen."

Her husband looked surprised, confounded, and knew not what to say. It was new to him, but not to me. I had witnessed such scenes before and believed that prayer had prevailed, nay, I felt sure of it in my own soul.

The work spread and prevailed until it began to exhibit unmistakable indications of the direction in which the Spirit of God was leading from that place. The distance to Rome was nine miles. About half way was a small village called Elmer's Hill. There was a large schoolhouse there where I held a weekly lecture, and it soon became evident that the work was spreading in the direction of Rome and Utica. There was a settlement about three miles northeast of Rome called Wright's settlement. Large numbers of persons from Rome and from Wright's settlement came down to attend the meetings at Elmer's Hill, and the work soon began to take effect among them.

There was one of my own experiences that, for the honor of God, I must not omit to relate in this connection. I had preached and prayed almost continually during the time that I had been at Mr. Gale's. As I was accustomed to use my voice in private prayer, for convenience' sake, that I might not be heard, I had spread a buffalo robe on the hayloft where I used to spend much of my time in secret prayer to God, when not abroad visiting or engaged in preaching. Mr. Gale had warned me several times that if I did not take care I would go beyond my strength and break down. But the Spirit of prayer was upon me and I would not resist him, but gave him scope and let out my strength freely in pouring out my soul to God.

It was November and the weather was becoming cold. Mr. Gale and I had been out with his horse and carriage, visiting inquirers. We came home, went into the barn and put out the horse. Instead of going into the house I crept up into the hayloft to pour out my burdened soul to God in prayer. I prayed until the burden left me. I was so exhausted that I fell asleep. I must have fallen asleep almost instantly, as I had no recollection of any time elapsing after the struggle in my soul was over.

The first I knew, Mr. Gale came climbing up into the hayloft and said, "Brother Finney, are you dead?" I awoke, and at first could form no idea how long I had been there. But this I knew, that my mind was

calm and my faith unwavering. The work would go
on, of that I felt assured.

14

At this time Rev. Moses Gillett, pastor of the Congregational church in Rome, hearing what the Lord was doing in Western, came with one of the prominent members of his church to see the work that was going on. They were both greatly impressed with the work of God. I could see that the Spirit of God was stirring them up to the deepest foundations of their minds. After a few days they came again, and on this second visit Mr. Gillett said to me, "Brother Finney, it seems to me that I have a new Bible. I never before understood the promises as I do now. I never got hold of them before. I cannot rest," he said. "My mind is full of the subject and the promises are new to me." This conversation led me to understand that the Lord was preparing him for a great work in his own congregation.

Soon after this, when the revival was in its full strength at Western, Mr. Gillett persuaded me to exchange a day with him. I consented reluctantly.

On the Saturday before the day of our exchange, on my way to Rome, I greatly regretted that I had consented to the exchange. I felt that it would greatly mar the work in Western, because Mr. Gillett would preach some of his old sermons, which I knew very well could not be adapted to the state of things. However, the people were praying and it would not stop the work, although it might retard it. I went to Rome and preached three times on Sunday. To me it was perfectly clear that the word took great effect. I could see during the day that many heads were down and that a great number of them were bowed down with deep conviction for sin. I preached in the morning on the text, "The carnal mind is enmity against God," and followed it up with something in the same direction in the afternoon and evening.

I waited on Monday morning until Mr. Gillett returned from Western. I told him what my impressions were in respect to the state of the people. He did not seem to realize that the work was beginning with such power as I supposed. But he wanted to call for inquirers, if there were any in the congregation, and wished me to be present at the meeting.

I have said before that the means that I had all along used, thus far, in promoting revivals were much prayer, secret and social, public preaching, personal conversation, and visitation from house to house; and when inquirers became multiplied I appointed meetings for them and invited those that were inquiring to meet for instruction, suited to their necessities. These were the only means I had thus far used in attempting to secure the conversion of souls.

Mr. Gillett asked me to be present at the proposed meeting of inquiry. I told him I would, and that he might circulate information through the village that there would be a meeting of inquiry on Monday evening. I would go to Western and return just at evening, it being understood that he was not to let the people know that he expected me to be present. The meeting was called at the house of one of his deacons.

When we arrived, we found the large sitting room crowded to its utmost capacity. Mr. Gillett looked around with surprise and considerable agitation, for he found that the meeting was composed of many of the most intelligent and influential members of his congregation and the prominent young men in the town.

We spent a little while in attempting to talk with them, and I soon saw that the feeling was so deep that there was danger of an outburst of feeling that would be almost uncontrollable. I therefore said to Mr. Gillett, "It will not do to continue the meeting in this shape. I will make some remarks, such as they need, and then dismiss them."

Nothing had been said or done to create any excitement in the meeting. The feeling was all spontaneous. The work was with such power that even a few words of conversation would make the stoutest men writhe in their seats, as if a sword had been thrust into their hearts. It would probably not be possible for one who had never witnessed such a scene to realize what force the truth sometimes has under the power of the Holy Spirit. It was indeed a sword, a two-edged sword. The pain that it produced when searchingly presented in a few words of conversation would create a distress that seemed unendurable.

Mr. Gillett became very much agitated. He turned pale and with a good deal of excitement said, "What shall we do? What shall we do?"

I put my hand on his shoulder and in a whisper said, "Keep quiet, keep quiet, brother Gillett." I then addressed them in as gentle but plain a manner as I could, calling their attention at once to their only remedy. I pointed them to Christ as the Savior of the world, and kept on in this strain as long as they could endure it, which, indeed, was but a few moments.

Mr. Gillett became so agitated that I stepped up to him and, taking him by the arm, said, "Let us pray." We knelt down in the middle of the room where we had been standing. I led in prayer, in a low, unimpassioned voice, but interceded with the Savior to interpose his blood, then and there, and to lead all these sinners to accept the salvation which he offered, and to believe to the saving of their souls.

The agitation deepened every moment, and as I could hear their sobs and sighs I closed my prayer and rose suddenly from my knees. They all rose and I said, "Now please go home without speaking a word to each other. Try to keep silent, and do not break out into any boisterous show of feeling, but go without saying a word, to your rooms."

At this moment a young man so nearly fainted that he fell upon some young men that stood near him, and they all partially swooned away and fell together. This had produced a loud shrieking, but I hushed them down and said to the young men, "Please set that door wide open and go out, and let us all leave in silence." They did as I requested. They were not loud, but they went out sobbing and sighing, and their sobs and sighs could be heard until they got out into the street.

The next morning, as soon as it was light, people began to call at Mr. Gillett's to have us go and visit members of their families, whom they represented as being under the greatest conviction. We ate a hasty breakfast and started out. As soon as we were in the streets the people ran out from many houses and begged us to go into their houses. As we could visit only one place at a time, when we went into a house the neighbors would rush in and fill the largest room. We would stay and give them instruction for a short time, and then go to another house, and the people would follow us.

We found a most extraordinary state of things. Convictions were so deep and universal that we would sometimes go into a house and find some in a kneeling posture and some prostrate on the floor. We visited, and conversed, and prayed in this manner, from house to house until noon. I then said to Mr. Gillett, "This will never do. We must have a meeting of inquiry. We cannot go from house to house, and we are not meeting the wants of the people at all." He agreed with me.

We went home and ate our lunch and started for the meeting. We saw people hurrying, some of them actually running to the meeting. They were coming from every direction. By the time we were there, the room, though a large one, was crammed to its utmost capacity. Men, women and children crowded the apartment.

This meeting was very much like the one we had had the night before. The feeling was overwhelming. Some men of the strongest nerves were so cut down by the remarks that were made that they were unable to help themselves and had to be taken home by their friends. This meeting lasted until nearly night. It resulted in a great number of hopeful conversions, and was the means of greatly extending the work on every side.

After this the work became so general that I preached every night for twenty nights in succession and twice on Sunday. Every day after the work had thus begun, we held a prayer meeting in the morning, a meeting for inquiry in the afternoon, with preaching in the evening.

Ministers came in from neighboring towns and expressed great astonishment at what they saw and heard, as well they might. Conversions multiplied so rapidly that we had no way of learning who were converted. Therefore every evening at the close of my sermon, I requested all who had been converted that day to come forward and report themselves in front of the pulpit that we might have a little conversation with them. Every night we were surprised by the number and the class of persons who came forward.

A physician, a very amiable man but a skeptic, had a little daughter and a praying wife. Little H——, a girl perhaps eight or nine years old, was strongly convicted of sin, and her mother was greatly interested in her state of mind. But her father was quite indignant.

He said to his wife, "The subject of religion is too high for me. I never could understand it. And do you tell me that that little child understands it so as to be intelligently convicted of sin? I do not believe it. I know better. I cannot endure it. It is fanaticism; it is madness."

Nevertheless the mother of the child held fast in prayer. The doctor made these remarks quite heatedly. Immediately afterward he took his horse and went several miles to see a patient. On his way, as he afterward remarked, that subject took possession of his mind in such manner that it was all opened to his understanding, and the whole plan of salvation by Christ was so clear to him that he saw that a child could understand it. He wondered that it had ever seemed so mysterious to him. He regretted exceedingly what he had said to his wife about little H——, and felt anxious to get home that he might take it back. He soon came home a changed man, told his wife what had passed in his own mind, and encouraged dear little H—— to come to Christ. Both father and daughter have since been earnest Christians and have lived long and done much good.

But in this revival, as in others that I have known, God did some terrible things in righteousness. On one Sunday while I was there, as we came out of the pulpit and were about to leave the church, a man came in haste to Mr. Gillett and myself and requested us to go to a certain place, saying that a man had fallen down dead there. I was engaged in conversing with somebody and Mr. Gillett went alone.

When I was through with the conversation I went to Mr. Gillett's house, and he soon returned and related this fact. Three men who had been opposing the work had met that Sunday and spent the day in drinking and ridiculing the work. They went on in this way until one of them suddenly fell dead. When Mr. Gillett arrived at the house and the circumstances were related to him, he said, "There! there is no doubt but that man has been stricken down by God and has been sent to hell." His companions were speechless. They could say nothing, for it was evident to them that their conduct had brought upon him this awful stroke of divine indignation.

As the work proceeded it gathered in nearly the whole population. Nearly every one of the lawyers, merchants, and physicians, and almost all the principal men, and indeed, nearly all the adult population of the village, were brought in, especially those who belonged to Mr. Gillett's congregation. He said to me before I left, "So far as my congregation is concerned the millennium is come already. My people are all converted. Of all my past labors I have not a sermon that is suited at all to my congregation, for they are all Christians." Mr. Gillett afterward reported that during the twenty days I spent at Rome, there were five hundred conversions in that town.

I should say a few words in regard to the spirit of prayer which prevailed at Rome at this time. Indeed the town was full of prayer. Go where you would, you heard the voice of prayer. Pass along the street, and if two or three Christians happened to be together, they were praying. Wherever they met they prayed. Wherever there was a sinner unconverted, especially if he showed any opposition, you would find some two or three brethren or sisters agreeing to make him a particular subject of prayer.

I think I should mention also the conversion of Mrs. Gillett during this revival. She was a beautiful woman, considerably younger than her husband, and his second wife. She had been, before Mr. Gillett married her, under conviction for several weeks and had become almost deranged. She had the impression that she was not one of the elect and that there was no salvation for her. Soon after the revival began in Rome she was powerfully convicted again by the Spirit of the Lord.

She was a woman of refinement and fond of dress, and as is very common wore about her head and on her person some trifling ornaments; nothing, however, that I would have thought of as being any stumbling block in her way at all. Being her guest, I talked repeatedly with her as her conviction increased, but it never occurred to me that her fondness for clothes could stand in the way of her being converted to God. But as the work became more powerful, her distress became alarming. Mr. Gillett, knowing what had formerly occurred in her case, felt quite alarmed lest she should get into that state of despondency in which she had been years before. She threw herself upon me for instruction. Almost every time I came into the house, she would come to me and beg me to pray for her, and tell me that her distress was more than she could bear. She was evidently going fast to despair, but I could see that she was depending too much on me; therefore I tried to avoid her.

It went on thus until one day I came into the house and went into the study. In a few moments, as usual, she was before me begging me to pray for her, and complaining that there was no salvation for her. I got up abruptly and left her without praying with her, saying to her that it was of no use for me to pray for her, that she was depending on my prayers. When I did so, she sank down as if she would faint. I left her alone, notwithstanding, and went abruptly from the study to the parlor.

In the course of a few moments she came rushing across the hall into the parlor, with her face all aglow, exclaiming, "Oh, Mr. Finney! I have found the Savior! I have found the Savior! Do you know it was the ornaments in my hair that stood in the way of my conversion? I have found when I prayed that they would come up before me, and I would be tempted to give them up. But I thought they were trifles and that God did not care about such trifles. This was a temptation of Satan. But the ornaments that I wore kept coming up continually before my mind whenever I attempted to give my heart to God. When you abruptly left me," she said, "I was driven to desperation. I cast myself down, and lo! these ornaments came up again, and I said, 'I will not have these things come up again. I will put them away from me forever.' I renounced them and hated them as things standing in the way of my salvation. As soon as I promised to give them up, the Lord revealed himself to my soul, and oh! I wonder why I have never understood this before! This was really the great difficulty with me before when I was under conviction, my fondness for clothes, and I did not know it."

15

When I had been at Rome about twenty days one of the elders of Mr. Aiken's church in Utica, a very prominent and useful man, died, and I went down to attend his funeral. Mr. Aiken conducted the funeral and I learned from him that the spirit of prayer was already evident in his congregation and in that city. He told me that one of his principal women had been so deeply exercised in her soul about the state of the church and the ungodly in that city that she had prayed for two days and nights almost incessantly until her strength was quite overcome. She could not endure the burden of her mind unless somebody was engaged in prayer with her, upon whose prayer she could lean, someone who could express her desires to God.

I understood this and told Mr. Aiken that the work had already begun in her heart. He recognized it, of course, and wished me to begin labor with him and his people immediately. I did so and the work began at once. The word took immediate effect and the place became filled with the manifested influence of the Holy Spirit. Our meetings were crowded every night and the work spread and went on powerfully, especially in the two Presbyterian congregations, one of which Mr. Aiken was pastor, and Mr. Brace of the other. I divided my labors between the two congregations.

It was in the midst of the revival in Utica that we

first heard of the opposition to those revivals that was
springing up in the East. One of the complaints was
that women would sometimes pray in the public meetings. It was true that in a few instances women—and
some very prominent women, who were strongly
pressed in spirit—would lead in prayer in the public
meetings which we held daily from house to house.
No opposition that I know of was shown to this either
in Utica or Rome. I had no part in introducing the
practice among the people and do not know whether
or not it had existed there before. Indeed, it was not
a subject of much conversation or thought in the neighborhood where it occurred. However, other complaints
were made and the opposition increased.

The work, however, went on with great power, converting all classes of people until Mr. Aiken reported
the hopeful conversion of five hundred in a few weeks.
Revivals were comparatively new in that region, and
the great mass of people had not become convinced that
they were the work of God. They were not awed by
them as they afterward became. It seemed to be extensively the impression that those revivals would soon
pass away and would prove to have been but mere
carnal excitement. Of course I do not mean that those
who were interested in the work had any such idea.

One circumstance occurred in the midst of that revival which made a powerful impression. The Oneida
presbytery met while the revival was going on in its
full strength. Among others there was an aged clergyman, a stranger to me, who was very much annoyed
by the heat and fervor of the revival. He found the
public mind all absorbed on the subject of religion and
that there was prayer and religious conversation everywhere, even in the stores and other public places. He
had never seen a revival and had never heard what
he heard there. He was a Scotchman and had not been
in this country very long.

On Friday afternoon before presbytery adjourned, he arose and made a violent speech against the revival while it was still going on. What he said greatly shocked and grieved the Christian people who were present. They felt like falling on their faces before God and crying to him to prevent what he had said from doing any mischief.

The presbytery adjourned just at evening. Some of the members went home and others remained overnight. Christians gave themselves to prayer. There was a great crying to God that night, that he would counteract any evil influence that might result from that speech. The next morning this man was found dead in his bed.

While making my home in Utica I preached frequently in New Hartford, a village four miles south of Utica. There was a precious and powerful work of grace there. I also preached at Whitesboro, another beautiful village four miles west of Utica, where there was also a powerful revival.

There was a cotton manufacturing plant on the Oriskany creek a little above Whitesboro, a place now called New York Mills. It was owned by an unconverted man, but a gentleman of high standing and good morals. My brother-in-law was at that time superintendent of the factory. I was invited to go and preach at that place and went up one evening and preached in the village schoolhouse, which was large and crowded with hearers. I could see that the word took powerful effect among the people, especially among the young people who were at work in the factory.

The next morning after breakfast I went into the factory to look through it. As I went through, I observed there was a good deal of agitation among those who were busy at their looms and spinning jennies*

---

*Machine for spinning several threads at the same time. Ed.

and other implements of work. On passing through one of the departments where a great number of young women were attending to their weaving, I observed a couple of them eyeing me and speaking very earnestly to each other. I could see that they were a good deal agitated, although they both laughed.

I went slowly toward them. They saw me coming and were evidently much excited. One of them was trying to mend a broken thread, but I observed that her hands trembled so that she could not mend it. I approached slowly, looking on each side at the machinery as I passed, but observed that this girl grew more and more agitated and could not proceed with her work. When I came within eight or ten feet of her I looked solemnly at her. She observed it and was quite overcome, and sank down and burst into tears. The impression caught like powder, and in a few moments nearly all in the room were in tears.

This feeling spread throughout the factory. The owner of the establishment was present and seeing the state of things he said to the superintendent, "Stop the mill and let the people attend to religion, for it is more important that our souls should be saved than that this factory run."

The gate was immediately shut and the factory stopped, but where should we assemble? The superintendent suggested that the spinning jenny room was large, and since the spinning jennies had been taken out, we could assemble there. We did so, and a more powerful meeting I scarcely ever attended. It went on with great power. The building was large and had many people in it, from the rafters to the cellar. The revival went through the mill with astonishing power, and in the course of a few days nearly all in the mill were converted.

The revival at Utica occurred in the winter and spring of 1826. When the converts had been received into the churches throughout the county, Rev. John Frost, pastor of the Presbyterian church at Whitesboro, published a pamphlet giving some account of the revival and stated that within the bounds of that presbytery the converts numbered three thousand. The work had spread from Rome and Utica as a center into every direction. Ministers came from a considerable distance and spent time in attending the meetings and in various ways helping forward the work. I spread my own labors over as large a field as I could. I cannot now remember all the places where I spent time. The pastors of all those churches sympathized deeply with the work, and like good and true men, laid themselves upon the altar and did all they could to forward the great and glorious movement. God gave them a rich reward.

From a letter which a prominent minister wrote about this time to a fellow pastor in New Haven, it appeared that someone had made the impression upon him that the brethren engaged in promoting these revivals were untruthful. In that letter he asserted that the spirit of lying was so predominant in those revivals that the brethren engaged in promoting them could not be at all believed. This letter found its way into print. If it should be republished at this day the people of the region where those revivals prevailed would think it very strange that this man should, even in a private letter, ever have written such things of the ministers and Christians engaged in promoting those great and wonderful revivals.

16

Dr. Lansing, pastor of the First Presbyterian Church at Auburn, came to Utica to witness the revival there and urged me to go out and labor for a time with him. In the summer of 1826 I complied with his request and went to labor with him for a season. Soon after I sent to Auburn I found that some of the professors from the theological seminary in that place were taking a hostile attitude toward the revival. I had known before that a considerable number of ministers east of Utica were corresponding with reference to these revivals and taking this attitude.

However, until I arrived at Auburn I was not fully aware of the amount of opposition I was destined to meet from the ministry, not the ministry in the region where I had labored but from ministers where I had not labored, who knew nothing personally of me but were influenced by the false reports which they heard. Soon after I arrived at Auburn I learned from various sources that a system of espionage was being carried on that was destined to result, and intended to result, in an extensive union of ministers and churches to hedge me in and prevent the spread of the revivals in connection with my labors.

Soon after I went to Auburn my mind became very much impressed with the extensive working of that system of espionage. Mr. Frost of Whitesboro knew the facts to a considerable extent and communicated them to me. I said nothing either publicly or privately that I remember to anybody on the subject, but gave myself to prayer. I looked to God with great earnestness day after day to be directed, asking him to show me the path of duty and give me grace to ride out the storm.

I shall never forget what a scene I passed through one day in my room at Dr. Lansing's. The Lord showed me as in a vision what was before me. He drew so near to me while I was engaged in prayer that my flesh literally trembled. I shook from head to foot under a full sense of the presence of God. At first, and for some time, it seemed more like being on the top of Sinai amidst its full thunderings than in the presence of the cross of Christ.

Never in my life that I can remember was I so awed and humbled before God. Nevertheless, instead of feeling like fleeing, I seemed drawn nearer and nearer to God—to that presence that filled me with such unutterable awe and trembling. After a season of great humiliation before him there came a great lifting up. God assured me that he would be with me and uphold me; that no opposition would prevail against me; that I had nothing to do in regard to all this matter but to keep about my work and wait for the salvation of God.

The sense of God's presence and all that passed between God and my soul at that time I can never describe. It led me to be perfectly trustful, perfectly calm, and to have nothing but the most perfectly kind feelings toward all the brethren that were misled and were arraying themselves against me. I felt assured that all would come out right; that my true course was to leave everything to God and to keep about my work. And as the storm gathered and the opposition increased, I never for one moment doubted how it would

result. I was never disturbed by it. I never spent a
waking hour in thinking of it even when to all outward appearance it seemed as if all the churches of
the land, except where I had labored, would unite to
shut me out of their pulpits. This was indeed the avowed
determination of the men that led in the opposition.
They were so deceived that they thought there was
no effective way but to unite and, as they expressed
it, "put him down." But God assured me that they
could not put me down.

A passage in Jeremiah was repeatedly set home
upon me with great power. It reads thus:

> O Lord, thou hast deceived me, and I was de-
> ceived: thou art stronger than I, and hast prevailed:
> I am in derision daily, every one mocketh me. For
> since I spoke, I cried out, I cried violence and spoil;
> because the word of the Lord was made a reproach
> unto me, and a derision, daily. Then I said, I will not
> make mention of him, nor speak any more in his
> name. But his word was in mine heart as a burning
> fire shut up in my bones, and I was weary with for-
> bearing, and I could not stay. For I heard the de-
> faming of many, fear on every side. Report, say
> they, and we will report it. All my familiars watched
> for my halting, saying, Peradventure he will be en-
> ticed, and we shall prevail against him, and we shall
> take our revenge on him.

> But the Lord is with me as a mighty terrible one:
> therefore my persecutors shall stumble, and they shall
> not prevail: they shall be greatly ashamed; for they
> shall not prosper: their everlasting confusion shall
> never be forgotten. But, O Lord of hosts, that triest
> the righteous, and seest the reins and the heart, let
> me see thy vengeance on them: for unto thee have
> I opened my cause. (Jer. 20:7-12)

I do not mean that this passage literally described
my case or expressed my feelings, but there was so
much similarity in the case that this passage was

often a support to my soul. The Lord did not allow me to take the opposition to heart, and I can truly say I never had an unkind feeling toward any leading opposer of the work during the whole of their opposition.

Notwithstanding the attitude that some of the theological professors at Auburn were taking in connection with so many ministers abroad, the Lord soon revived his work in Auburn. Mr. Lansing had a large congregation and a very intelligent one. The revival soon took effect among the people and became powerful.

There was a hatter residing at this time in Auburn. His wife was a Christian, but he believed in universal salvation and was an opposer of the revival. He carried his opposition so far as to forbid his wife to attend our meetings, and for several successive nights she remained at home.

One night as the bell rang for the meeting half an hour before the assembly met, she became so exercised in mind about her husband that she retired for prayer and spent the half hour pouring out her soul to God. She told him how her husband behaved, that he would not let her attend the meetings, and she drew very near to God.

As the bell began ringing for the people to assemble, she came out of her closet, as I later learned, and found that her husband had come in from the shop. As she entered the sitting room he asked her if she would not like to go to the meeting, and said that if she would go he would accompany her.

He afterward informed me that he had made up his mind to attend the meeting that night to see if he could get something to justify his opposition to his wife, or at least something to laugh about and sustain him in ridiculing the whole work. When he proposed to accompany his wife, she was very surprised but prepared herself and they came to the meeting.

Of all this I knew nothing at the time, of course. I had been visiting and laboring with inquirers the whole day, and had had no time whatever to arrange my thoughts, or even settle upon a text. During the introductory services a text occurred to my mind. It was the words of the man with the unclean spirit who cried out, "Let us alone!" I took those words and went on to preach, endeavoring to show the conduct of those sinners who wanted to be left alone, who did not want to have anything to do with Christ.

The Lord gave me power to give a very vivid description of the course that class of men were pursuing. In the midst of my discourse, I observed a person fall from his seat near the center aisle and cry out in a most terrific manner. The congregation was shocked. The outcry of the man was so great that I stopped preaching and stood still.

After a few moments I requested the congregation to sit still while I would go down and speak with the man. I found him to be this hatter of whom I have been speaking. The Spirit of the Lord had so powerfully convicted him that he was unable to sit on his seat. When I reached him, he had recovered his strength enough to be on his knees with his head in his wife's lap. He was weeping aloud like a child, confessing his sins and accusing himself in a terrible manner. I said a few words to him, to which he seemed to pay but little attention. The Spirit of God had his attention so thoroughly that I soon desisted from all efforts to make him listen to what I said.

When I told the congregation who it was, they all knew him and his character, and it produced tears and sobs in every part of the house. I stood for some little time to see if he would be quiet enough for me to go on with my sermon, but his loud weeping made it impossible. I can never forget the appearance of his wife as she sat and held his face in her hands upon her lap. There appeared in her face a holy joy and triumph that words cannot express.

We had several prayers, and then I dismissed the meeting. Some persons helped him to his house. He immediately wished them to send for certain of his companions with whom he had been in the habit of ridiculing the work of the Lord in that place. He could not rest until he had sent for a great number of them and had made confession to them, which he did with a very broken heart.

He was so overcome that for two or three days he could not get about town and continued to send for such men as he wished to see that he might confess to them and warn them to flee from the wrath to come. As soon as he was able to get about, he took hold of the work with the utmost humility and simplicity of character, but with great earnestness. Soon after, he was made an elder and since then he has been a very exemplary and useful Christian. His conversion was so marked and so powerful, and the results were so evident, that it did very much to silence the opposition.

There were several wealthy men in the town who took offense at Dr. Lansing and me and the laborers in that revival. After I left they got together and formed a new congregation. Most of these were unconverted men at the time. Let the reader bear this in mind, for in its proper place I shall have occasion to note the results of this opposition and the formation of a new congregation, and the subsequent conversion of nearly every one of those opposers.

Soon after my arrival at Auburn a circumstance occurred of so striking a character that I must give a brief account of it. My wife and I were guests of Dr. Lansing, the pastor of the church. The church was much conformed to the world and was accused by the unconverted of being leaders in dress, and fashion,

and worldliness. As usual I directed my preaching to
secure the reformation of the church and to get them
into a revival state. One Sunday I preached as searchingly as I was able to the church in regard to their
attitude before the world. The word took deep hold
of the people.

At the close of my address I called, as usual, upon
the pastor to pray. He was much impressed with the
sermon and instead of immediately engaging in prayer,
he made a short but very earnest address to the church,
confirming what I had said to them.

At this moment a man arose in the balcony and
said in a very deliberate and distinct manner, "Mr.
Lansing, I do not believe that such remarks from you
can do any good while you wear a ruffled shirt and
a gold ring, and while your wife and the ladies of your
family sit, as they do, before the congregation dressed
as leaders in the fashions of the day."

It seemed as if this would kill Dr. Lansing outright.
He made no reply, but cast himself across the side
of the pulpit and wept like a child. The congregation
was almost as shocked and affected as himself. They
almost universally dropped their heads upon the seat
in front of them, and many of them wept on every
side. With the exception of the sobs and sighs, the
house was profoundly silent. I waited a few moments,
and as Dr. Lansing did not move, I arose and offered
a short prayer and dismissed the congregation.

I went home with the dear, wounded pastor, and
when all the family were returned from church he
took the ring from his finger. It was a slender gold
ring that could hardly attract notice. He said that his
first wife, when upon her dying bed, took it from her
finger and placed it upon his, with a request that he
should wear it for her sake. He had done so without
a thought of its being a stumbling block. Of his ruffles,
he said he had worn them from his childhood and did

not think of them as anything improper. Indeed, he could not remember when he began to wear them, and of course thought nothing about them. "But," he said, "if these things are an occasion of offense to any, I will not wear them." He was a precious Christian man and an excellent pastor.

Almost immediately after this the church was disposed to make to the world a public confession of their backsliding and lack of a Christian spirit. Accordingly a confession was drawn up, covering the whole ground. It was submitted to the church for their approval, and then read before the congregation. The church arose and stood, many of them weeping while the confession was read. From this point the work went forward, with greatly increased power. The confession was evidently a heart-work and no sham. God most graciously accepted it and the mouths of the accusers were shut.

17

Early in the autumn of this year, 1826, I accepted an invitation to labor in Troy. I spent the fall and winter there, and the revival was powerful in that city. While there I was the guest of a judge. His father was living with him at the time. The old gentleman had been a judge in Vermont. He was remarkably correct in his outward life, a venerable man whose house in Vermont had been the home of ministers who visited the place. He was to all appearance quite satisfied with his amiable and self-righteous life. His wife had told me of her anxiety for his conversion, and his son had repeatedly expressed fear that his father's self-righteousness would never be overcome and that his natural amiability would ruin his soul.

One Sunday morning the Holy Spirit opened the case to my understanding and showed me how to reach it. In a few moments I had the whole subject in my mind. I went downstairs and told the lady and her son what I was about to do and asked them to pray earnestly for him. I followed out what the Lord had shown me, and the word took such powerful hold of him that he spent a sleepless night. His wife informed me that he had spent a night of anguish, that his self-righteousness was thoroughly annihilated, and that he was almost in despair. His son had told me that he had long prided himself on being better than other members of the church. He soon became clearly converted and lived a Christian life to the end.

I must mention a little incident connected somewhat with the opposition that had been shown at Troy. The presbytery of Columbia had a meeting, somewhere within its bounds, while I was in that area. Being informed that I was laboring in one of their churches, they appointed a committee to visit the place and inquire into the state of things, for they had been led to believe, from the opposition of others, that my method of conducting revivals was so very objectionable that it was the duty of the presbytery to inquire into it. They appointed two of their number to visit the place. It was feared that it might create some division and make some disturbance if the committee came. Some of the most engaged Christians made this a particular subject of prayer, and for a day or two before the time when they were expected they prayed much that the Lord would overrule this thing and not allow it to divide the church or introduce any element of discord. The committee was expected to be there on Sunday and attend the meetings. But the day before, a violent snowstorm set in. The snow fell so deep that they found it impossible to get through, were detained over Sunday, and on Monday found their way back to their own congregations.

Soon after this I received a letter from another minister informing me that the presbytery had appointed him one of a committee to visit me and make some inquiry in regard to my method of conducting revivals. He invited me to come and spend a Sunday with him and preach for him. I did so. As I understood afterward, his report to the presbytery was that it was unnecessary for them to take any further action in the case, that the Lord was in the work and they should take heed lest they be found fighting against God. I heard no more of opposition from that source. I have never doubted that the presbytery of Columbia was honestly alarmed at what they had heard. I have never called in question the propriety of the course which they took, and I admired their honesty in receiving testimony from proper sources. So far as I know they thereafter sympathized with the work that was going on.

That the brethren who opposed those revivals were good men, I do not doubt. That they were misled and grossly and most injuriously deceived, I have just as little doubt. I bless the Lord that I was kept from being diverted from my work by their opposition and that I never gave myself any uneasiness about it. I cannot be too thankful that God kept me from being agitated or changed in my spirit or views of labor by all the opposition of those days.

Soon after the adjournment of the convention, one Sunday as I came out of the pulpit a young lady by the name of S—— from Stephentown was introduced to me. She asked me if I could go up to their town and preach. I replied that my hands were full and that I did not see that I could. I saw her words were choked with deep feeling, but as I had not time to talk with her then I went to my lodging.

On the next Sunday Miss S—— met me again as I came out of the pulpit and begged me to go up to Stephentown and preach. She asked if I knew anything of the state of things there. I informed her that I did, but I told her I did not know how I could go. She appeared greatly affected, too much so to talk, for she could not control her feelings. These facts, together with what I had heard, began to take hold of me.

I finally told her that if the elders of the church desired me to come, she might have a notice given out that I would come up, Lord willing, and preach in their church the next Sunday at five o'clock in the afternoon. This would allow me to preach twice where I was, after which I could ride up to Stephentown. This seemed to light up her countenance and lift the load from her heart. She went home and had the notice given.

Accordingly the next Sunday after preaching the second time, one of the new converts offered to take me up to Stephentown in his carriage. When he came to take me I asked him, "Have you a steady horse?"

"Oh, yes!" he replied, "perfectly so," and smiling, he asked, "What made you ask the question?"

"Because," I replied, "if the Lord wants me to go to Stephentown the devil will prevent it if he can, and if you do not have a steady horse, he will try to make him kill me."

He smiled and we rode on. Strange to tell, before we got there that horse ran away twice and came near killing us. His owner expressed the greatest astonishment and said he had never known such a thing before.

However, in due time we arrived in safety at Mr. S——'s, the father of Miss S—— whom I have mentioned. He lived about half a mile from the church. As we went in we met Maria—for that was her name— who tearfully, yet joyfully, received us and showed me to a room where I could be alone, as it was not quite time for the meeting. Soon after I heard her praying in a room over my head. When it was time for the meeting, we all went and found a very large gathering. The congregation was solemn and attentive, but nothing very particular occurred that evening. I spent the night at Mr. S——'s, and this Maria seemed to be praying over my room nearly all night. I could hear her low, trembling voice, interrupted often by sobs and open weeping. I had made no appointment to come again, but before I left in the morning she pled so hard that I consented to speak at five o'clock the next Sunday.

When I came the next Sunday nearly the same things occurred as before, but the congregation was more crowded, and as the building was old, for fear the bal-

conies would break down they had been strongly
propped during the week. I could see a distinct increase
of solemnity and interest the second time I preached
there. I then left an appointment to preach again. At
the third service the Spirit of God was poured out on
the congregation.

The state of things in Stephentown now demanded
that I should take up my quarters there. I did so. The
spirit of prayer in the meantime had come powerfully
upon me, as had been the case for some time with
Miss S——. The praying power so greatly spreading
and increasing, the work soon took on a very powerful
type, so much so that the word of the Lord would cut
the strongest men down and render them entirely help-
less. I could name many cases of this kind.

The preceding summer Rev. Gilbert of Wilmington,
Delaware, came to Stephentown for a visit. Mr. Gilbert
was very old-school in his theological views, but a good
and earnest man. He heard me preach and saw the
results, and was very earnest that I should come and
aid him in Wilmington.

As soon as I could see my way to leave Stephentown,
therefore, I went to Wilmington and engaged in labors
with Mr. Gilbert. I soon found that his teaching had
placed the church in a position that made it impossible to promote a revival among them until their views
could be corrected. It was plain that nothing could
be done unless Mr. Gilbert's views could first be
changed upon this subject. I therefore spent hours each
day in conversing with him on his peculiar views. We
talked the subject all over in a brotherly manner, and
after laboring with him in this way for two or three
weeks, I saw that his mind was prepared to have my
own views brought before his people.

The next Sunday I took for my text "Make to yourselves a new heart and a new spirit; for why will you
die?" I went thoroughly into the subject of the sinner's

responsibility, and showed what a new heart is not, and what it is. I preached about two hours and did not sit down until I had gone over the whole subject as thoroughly as my rapid speaking would enable me to do in that length of time. The congregation became intensely interested, and great numbers rose and stood on their feet in every part of the house, which was completely filled. Some looked distressed and offended, others intensely interested. Some laughed, some wept, some were obviously angry, but no one left the house. It was a strange excitement.

In the meantime, Mr. Gilbert moved himself from one end of the sofa to the other in the pulpit behind me. I could hear him breathe and sigh, and could not help observing that he was himself in the greatest anxiety. But I was preaching to please the Lord and not man. I thought that it might be the last time I should ever preach there, but purposed at all events to tell them the whole truth on the subject, whatever the result might be.

When I was through I did not call upon Mr. Gilbert to pray, for I dared not. I prayed myself that the Lord would set home the word, make it understood, and give a candid mind to weigh what had been said, to receive the truth and reject what might be erroneous. I then dismissed the assembly and went down the pulpit stairs, Mr. Gilbert following me.

As I came down the pulpit stairs I observed two ladies sitting on the left hand of the aisle through which we must pass, who I knew were particular friends and supporters of Mr. Gilbert. I saw that they looked partly grieved, partly offended, and greatly astonished. The first we reached, who was near the pulpit stairs, took hold of Mr. Gilbert as he was following behind me and said to him, "Mr. Gilbert, what do you think of that?" She spoke in a loud whisper.

He replied in the same manner, "It is worth five hundred dollars." That greatly gratified me and affected me very much.

She replied, "Then you have never preached the Gospel."

"Well," said he, "I am sorry to say I never have."

We passed along, and then the other lady said to him about the same things and received a similar reply.

That was enough for me. I made my way to the door and went out. As I passed along the streets going to Mr. Gilbert's, where I lodged, I found the streets full of excitement and discussion. I saw that the impression was decidedly in favor of what had been said.

When I arrived at Mr. Gilbert's, his wife accosted me as soon as I entered by saying, "Mr. Finney, how dared you preach any such thing in our pulpit?"

I replied, "Mrs. Gilbert, I did not dare to preach anything else; it is the truth of God."

She replied, "Well, if the doctrine preached by Mr. Gilbert was true, God was under obligation as a matter of justice to make an atonement and to save me from those circumstances in which it was impossible for me to help myself and from a condemnation which I did not deserve."

Just at this moment Mr. Gilbert entered. "There," said I, "brother Gilbert, you see the results of your preaching here in your own family," and then repeated to him what his wife had just said. "She has always thought that God owed her, as a matter of justice, the salvation provided in Christ. How can she be a Christian?"

Upon my making the last remark, she got up and left the room. For two days I did not see her. She then came out clear, not only in the truth but in the state of her own mind, having passed through a complete revolution of views and experience.

From this point the work went forward. The truth was worked out admirably by the Holy Spirit. Mr. Gilbert's views became greatly changed as well as his style of preaching and manner of presenting the Gospel.

18

In the meantime I had been induced to preach for Mr. Patterson at Philadelphia, twice each week. I went on the steamboat and preached in the evening, and then returned the next day and preached at Wilmington, thus alternating my evening services between Wilmington and Philadelphia. The distance was about forty miles. The word took so much effect in Philadelphia that I soon felt it my duty to leave Mr. Gilbert to carry on the work in Wilmington and give my whole time to labor in Philadelphia.

Rev. James Patterson, with whom I first labored in Philadelphia, held the views of theology then held at Princeton, since known as the theology of the old school Presbyterian. But he was a godly man and cared a great deal more for the salvation of souls than for any of those points of doctrine between the old and the new school Presbyterian. It will be remembered that at this time I belonged to the Presbyterian church myself. I had been licensed and ordained by a presbytery, composed mostly of men educated at Princeton.

The revival took such hold in his congregation as greatly to interest him, and when he saw that God was blessing the word as I presented it, he stood firmly by me and never objected to anything that I advanced. Sometimes when we returned from the meeting, Mrs. Patterson would smilingly remark, "Now you see, Mr.

Patterson, that Mr. Finney does not agree with you on those points upon which we have so often conversed."

He would always, in the greatness of his Christian faith and love, reply, "Well, the Lord blesses it."

The interest became so great that our congregations were packed at every meeting. One day Mr. Patterson said to me, "Brother Finney, if the Presbyterian ministers in this city find out your views, and what you are preaching to the people, they will hunt you out of the city as they would a wolf."

I replied, "I cannot help it. I can preach no other doctrine. If they must drive me out of the city, let them do it and take the responsibility. But I do not believe that they can get me out." However, the ministers did not take the course that he predicted by any means, but nearly all received me to their pulpits.

As in other places, there were some cases of very bitter opposition on the part of individuals. In one case, a man whose wife was very deeply convicted was so enraged that he came in and took his wife out of the meeting by force. Another case was of a German who was a tobacconist. He had a very amiable and intelligent wife, but he was a skeptic and had no confidence in religion at all. His wife came to our meetings, and after a severe inner struggle of many days, she was thoroughly converted. Her husband soon began to oppose her being a Christian. He had a hasty temper, was a man of athletic build, and of great resolution and fixedness of purpose. His opposition increased until he finally forbade his wife attending meetings any more.

She then called to see me and asked my advice with regard to what course she should take. I told her that her first obligation was to God. In accordance with my advice she attended the meetings as she had opportunity and soon came into the liberty of the Gospel with great peace of mind, and enjoyed much the presence of God. This highly displeased her husband, and he finally went so far as to threaten her life if she went to the meeting again. She told him calmly that whatever it cost her, her mind was made up to do her duty to God.

One Sunday evening when she returned from the meeting she found him in a great rage. As soon as she entered the door he locked it after her, took out the key, and then drew a dagger and swore to take her life. She ran upstairs. He grabbed a light to follow her, but the servant girl blew out the light as he passed by her. This left them all in the dark. His wife ran through the rooms in the second story, found her way down into the kitchen, into the cellar and out a cellar window. He could not follow her in the dark. She went to a friend's house and spent the night.

Taking it for granted that he would be ashamed of his rage before morning she went home early, entered her house and found things in the greatest disorder. He had broken some of the furniture and acted like a man greatly disturbed. He again locked the door as soon as she was fairly in the house, drew a dagger and took the most horrible oath that he would take her life. She ran upstairs, but it was light and he followed her. She ran from room to room until finally she entered the last, from which there was no escape. She turned around and faced him. She threw herself upon her knees as he was about to strike her with his dagger. She lifted up her hands to heaven and cried for mercy upon herself and upon him. At this point God arrested him. Her husband looked at her for a moment, dropped his dagger, fell upon the floor and cried for mercy himself. He broke down, confessed his sins to God and to her, and begged God, and begged her, to forgive him. From that moment he was a wonderfully changed man. He became one of the most earnest Christian converts and was greatly attached to me.

I found Mr. Patterson to be one of the truest and holiest men that I have ever labored with. His preaching was quite remarkable. He was a tall man, of striking figure and powerful voice. He would preach with the tears rolling down his cheeks and with an earnestness and pathos that were very striking. I only heard him preach occasionally, and when I first did so I was pained, thinking that his rambling nature of preaching could not take effect. However, I was mistaken. Notwithstanding his rambling, his great earnestness and anointing fastened the truth on the hearts of his hearers, and I never heard him preach without finding some persons deeply convicted by what he said. I respect and reverence his very name. He was a lovely Christian man and a faithful minister of Jesus Christ.

After preaching in Mr. Patterson's church for several months and in nearly all the Presbyterian churches in the city, it was thought best that I should take up a central position and preach steadily in one place. The elders of a large German church, together with their pastor, requested me to occupy their pulpit. Their house was the largest house of worship in the city, seating three thousand people. It was always crowded. There I preached steadily for several months. In all this time there was no abatement of the revival that I could see. Converts became numerous in every part of the city.

In the spring of 1829 when the Delaware River was high, lumbermen came down with their rafts from the region of the high land where they had been cutting timber. Many persons were engaged in getting out lumber, summer and winter. It was floated down to Philadelphia in the spring of the year.

Many of the lumbermen were raising families in that northern region of Pennsylvania where there was a large tract of country unsettled and unoccupied, except by these lumbermen. They had no schools and no churches or religious privileges at all. I knew a minister who told me he was born in that lumber region, and that when he was twenty years old he had never attended a religious meeting and did not know the alphabet.

These men that came down with lumber attended our meetings, and quite a number of them were hopefully converted. They went back into the wilderness and began to pray for the outpouring of the Holy Spirit, to tell the people around them what they had seen in Philadelphia, and to exhort them to attend to their salvation. Their efforts were immediately blessed, and the revival began to take hold and to spread among those lumbermen. It spread to such an extent that in many cases persons would be convicted and converted who had not attended any meetings, and were almost completely ignorant. Men who were getting out lumber and were living alone in little shanties, or where two or three or more were together, would be seized with such conviction that it would lead them to wander off and inquire what they should do. They would be converted and thus the revival spread.

One man, for example, had a little shanty by himself where he slept at night, getting out his shingles during the day. He began to feel that he was a sinner. His convictions increased upon him until he broke down, confessed his sins and repented, and the Spirit of God revealed to him so much of the way of salvation that he evidently knew the Savior. But he had never attended a prayer meeting or heard a prayer in his life. His feelings became such that he finally felt constrained to go and tell some of his acquaintances that were getting out lumber in another place, how he felt. But when he arrived, he found that a good many of them felt just as he did and that they were holding prayer meetings. He attended their prayer meetings, heard them pray, and finally prayed himself. This was the form of his prayer: "Lord, you have got me down and I hope you will keep me down. And since you have had such good luck with me, I hope you will try other sinners."

This work began in the spring of 1829. In the spring of 1831 two or three men from this lumber region came to inquire how they could get some ministers to go up there. They said that not less than five thousand people had been converted in that lumber region, that the revival had extended itself along for eighty miles, and there was not a single minister of the gospel there. I have never been in that region, but from all I have ever heard about it, I have regarded that as one of the most remarkable revivals that have occurred in this country. It was carried on almost independently of the ministry, among a class of people very ignorant in regard to all ordinary instruction; and yet so clear and wonderful were the teachings of God that the revival was remarkably free from fanaticism, or wildness, or anything that was objectionable. The spark that was struck into the hearts of those few lumbermen that came to Philadelphia spread over that forest and resulted in the salvation of a multitude of souls.

19

I returned to Oneida County, New York, about mid-summer, 1830, and spent a short time at my father-in-law's. While there a messenger came from the town of Columbia requesting me to go down and assist a work of grace there which had already begun. I felt I should go but did not expect to remain there, as I had other more pressing calls for labor. I went down, however, to see and to lend such aid as I was able for a short time.

At Columbia there was a large German church, the membership of which had been received upon examination of their doctrinal knowledge instead of their Christian experience. Thus the church had been composed mostly of unconverted persons. Both the church and the congregation were large. Their pastor was a young man of German descent from Pennsylvania.

He told me he had studied theology with a German doctor of divinity who did not encourage experiential religion at all. One of his fellow students was religiously inclined and used to pray in his closet. Their teacher suspected this and in some way came to a knowledge of the fact. He warned the young man against it as a very dangerous practice, said he would become insane if he persisted in it, and that he would be blamed himself for allowing a student to take such a course.

The pastor said that he himself had had no religion.

He had joined the church in the common way and had no thought that anything else was required, so far as piety was concerned, to become a minister. But his mother was a pious women. She knew better and was greatly distressed that a son of hers who had never been converted should enter the sacred ministry. When he had received a call to the church in Columbia and was about to leave home, his mother had a very serious talk with him, impressed upon him the fact of his responsibility, and said some things that bore powerfully upon his conscience. He said he could not forget this conversation with his mother. It bore upon his mind heavily, and his convictions of sin deepened until he was nearly in despair.

This continued for many months. He had no one to consult, and did not open his mind to anybody. But after a severe and long struggle he was converted, came into the light, saw where he was, where he had been, and saw the condition of his church and of all those churches which had admitted their members in the way he had been admitted. His wife was unconverted. He immediately gave himself to labor for her conversion, and under God, he soon secured it. His soul was full of the subject, and he read his Bible and prayed and preached with all his might. But he was a young convert and had no instruction such as he needed, so felt at a loss what to do. He rode about the town and conversed with the elders of the church and with the leading members, and satisfied himself that one or two of the elders and several of his women members knew what it was to be converted.

After much prayer and consideration he made up his mind what to do. On Sunday he gave them notice that there would be a meeting of the church on a certain day during the week for the transaction of business, and wished all the church to be present. His own conversion, preaching, visiting, and conversing around the town had already created a good deal of excitement so that religion came to be the common topic of conversation. His call for a church meeting was responded to so that on the day appointed nearly all the church members were present.

He then addressed them in regard to the real state of the church and the error they had fallen into in regard to the conditions on which members had been received. He made a speech to them, partly in German and partly in English, so as to have all classes understand as far as he could. After talking until they were a good deal moved, he proposed to disband the church and form a new one, insisting that this was essential to the prosperity of religion. He had an understanding with those members of the church, whom he was satisfied were truly converted, that they should lead in voting for the disbanding of the church. The motion was put; whereupon the converted members arose as requested. They were very influential members, and the people looking around and seeing these on their feet rose up, and finally they kept rising until the vote was nearly unanimous. The pastor then said, "There is now no church in Columbia, and we propose to form one of Christians, of people who have been converted."

He then, before the congregation, related his own experience, and called on his wife and she did the same. Then the converted elders and members followed, one after another, as long as any could come forward and relate a Christian experience. These they proceeded to form into a church. He then said to the others, "Your church relations are dissolved. You are out in the world, and until you are converted and in the church, you cannot partake of the ordinances of the church, nor have your children baptized." This created a great panic, for according to their views it was an awful thing not to partake of the sacrament and not to have their children baptized, for this was the way in which they themselves had been made member "Christians."

The pastor then labored with all his might. He visited and preached and prayed and held meetings, and the interest increased. Thus the work had been going on for some time when he heard that I was in Oneida County and sent for me. I found him a warmhearted young convert. He listened to my preaching with almost irrepressible joy. I found the congregation large and interested, and so far as I could judge, the work was in a very prosperous, healthful state. That revival continued to spread until it reached and converted nearly all the inhabitants of the town. Galesburg, Illinois, was settled by a group of believers from Columbia who were nearly all converts of the revival. The founder of the church and of Knox College, located there, was Mr. Gale, my former pastor at Adams.

Not long after, I was invited to visit the city of New York. Anson G. Phelps, since well known as a great contributor to the leading benevolent institutions of our country through his will, hearing that I had not been invited to the pulpits of that city, hired a vacant church and sent me an urgent request to come there and preach. I did so, and there we had a powerful revival. I found Mr. Phelps very much engaged in the work and not hesitating at any expense that was necessary to promote it.

During my labors there I was very struck with the piety of Mr. Phelps. For a time I and my wife, with our only child, were guests in his family. I had observed that while Mr. Phelps was a man literally loaded with business, somehow he preserved a highly spiritual frame of mind. He would come directly from his business to our prayer meetings, and enter into them with such spirit as to show clearly that his mind was not absorbed in business to the exclusion of spiritual things. As I watched him from day to day I became more and more interested in his interior life, as it was made evident in his outward life.

One night I had occasion to go downstairs, about twelve or one o'clock at night, to get something for our little child. I supposed the family were all asleep, but to my surprise I found Mr. Phelps sitting by his fire in his nightshirt, and saw that I had broken in upon his secret devotions. I apologized by saying that I supposed he was in bed.

He replied, "Brother Finney, I have a great business pressing me during the day, and have but little time for secret devotion. My custom is, after having a nap at night, to arise and have a season of communion with God."

After his death, which occurred not many years ago, it was found that he had kept a journal during these hours in the night comprising several manuscript volumes. This journal revealed the secret workings of his mind and the real progress of his interior life.

In giving my narrative of revivals thus far I have passed over a great number of cases of crime, committed by persons who came to me for advice and told me the facts. In many instances in these revivals, restitution, sometimes to the amount of many thousands of dollars, was made by those whose consciences troubled them, either because they had obtained the money directly by fraud, or by some selfish overreaching in their business relations.

A young woman in New York visited me one day under great conviction of sin. In talking with her I found that she had many things upon her conscience. From her childhood, she had been in the habit of stealing. She was the daughter and only child of a widow and had been in the habit of taking handkerchiefs, jewelry, pencils and whatever she had an opportunity to steal from her schoolmates and others. She made confession concerning some of these things to me and asked me what she should do about it. It told her she must return them and make confession to those from whom she had stolen.

This of course greatly tried her, yet her convictions were so deep that she dare not keep them, and she began the work of making confession and restitution. But as she went forward with it, she continued to recall more and more instances of the kind, and kept visiting me frequently and confessing to me her thefts of almost every kind of articles that a young woman could use. I asked her if her mother knew that she had these things.

She said yes, but that she had always told her mother that they were given to her. She said to me on one occasion, "Mr. Finney, I suppose I have stolen a million times. I find I have many things that I know I stole, but I cannot remember from whom."

I refused altogether to compromise with her, and insisted on her making restitution in every case in which she could by any means recall the facts. From time to time she would come to me and report what she had done. I asked her what the people said when she returned the articles. She replied, "Some of them say that I am crazy; some of them say that I am a fool; and some of them are very much affected."

"Do they all forgive you?" I asked.

"Oh, yes! They all forgive me, but some of them think that I had better not do as I am doing."

One day she informed me that she had a shawl which she had stolen from a daughter of the Bishop of New York. As usual, I told her that she must restore it. A few days later she called and told me the result. She said she folded up the shawl in a paper, went with it and rang the bell at the bishop's door. When the servant came she handed him the bundle directed to the bishop. She made no explanation but turned immediately away and ran around the corner into another street, lest someone should look out and see which way she went and find out who she was. But after she got around the corner her conscience smote her and she said to herself, "I have not done this thing right. Somebody else may be suspected of having stolen the shawl unless I tell the bishop who did it."

She turned around, went immediately back and asked if she could see the bishop. Being informed that she could, she was conducted into his study. She then confessed to him, told him about the shawl, and all that had passed.

"Well," said I, "and how did the bishop receive you?"

"Oh," she said, "when I told him he wept, laid his hand on my head, forgave me, and prayed God to forgive me."

"And have you been at peace in your mind about that transaction since?"

"Oh, yes!" she said.

This process continued for weeks and perhaps months. This girl was going from place to place in all parts of the city, restoring things that she had stolen, and making confession. Sometimes her convictions would be so awful it seemed as if she would become insane.

One morning she sent for me to come to her mother's house. I did so, and when I arrived I was taken to her room and found her with her hair hanging over her shoulders and her clothes in disorder, walking the room in an agony of despair with a look that was frightful, because it indicated that she might well be losing her mind. I said, "My dear child, what is the matter?"

She held in her hand, as she was walking, a little Testament. She turned to me and said, "Mr. Finney, I stole this Testament. I have stolen God's Word, and will God ever forgive me? I cannot remember which of the girls it was that I stole it from. I stole it from one of my schoolmates, and it was so long ago that I had really forgotten that I had stolen it. It occurred to me this morning, and it seems to me that God can never forgive me for stealing his Word."

I assured her that there was no reason for her despair. "But," she said, "what shall I do? I cannot remember where I got it."

I told her, "Keep it as a constant reminder of your former sins, and use it for the good you may now get from it."

"Oh," she said, "if I could only remember where I got it, I would instantly give it back."

"Well, if you ever remember where you got it, make an instant restitution, either by restoring that, or by giving another as good."

"I will!" she promised.

All this process was exceedingly affecting to me, but as it proceeded, the state of mind that resulted from these transactions was truly wonderful. A depth of humility, a deep knowledge of herself and her own depravity, a brokenness of heart and repentance of spirit, and finally, a faith and joy and love and peace like a river followed. She became one of the most delightful young Christians I have known.

When the time drew near that I expected to leave New York, I thought that someone in the church who could watch over her ought to be acquainted with her. Up to this time whatever had passed between us had been a secret, sacredly kept to myself. But as I was about to leave I narrated the fact to Mr. Phelps, and the narration affected him greatly.

He said, "Brother Finney, introduce me to her. I will be her friend. I will watch over her for her good." He did so, as I afterward learned. For many years the woman has had a consistent Christian character and is known as an excellent praying woman.

20

Leaving New York I spent a few weeks at my father-in-law's, and, as was common, being pressed to go in many directions, I was greatly at a loss as to what was my duty. But among others, an urgent invitation was received from a Presbyterian church in Rochester. I inquired into the circumstances and found that on several accounts it was a very unpromising field of labor.

With these pressing invitations before me, I felt, as I have often done, greatly perplexed. I remained at my father-in-law's and considered the subject until I felt that I must take hold and work somewhere. Accordingly we packed our trunks and went down to Utica, about seven miles distant, where I had many praying friends. We arrived there in the afternoon, and in the evening quite a number of the leading brethren, in whose prayers and wisdom I had a great deal of confidence, at my request met for consultation and prayer in regard to my next field of labor. I laid all the facts before them in regard to Rochester, and so far as I was acquainted with them, the leading facts in respect to the other fields to which I was invited at that time. Rochester seemed to be the least inviting of them all.

After talking the matter over and having several seasons of prayer, they were unanimous in the opinion that Rochester was too uninviting a field of labor. They were firm in the conviction that I should go east from Utica and not west. At the time this was my own impression and conviction, and I retired from this meeting, settled not to go to Rochester but to New York or Philadelphia. This was before railroads existed, and when we parted that evening I expected to take the canal boat, which was the most convenient way for a family to travel, and to start in the morning for New York.

But after I retired to my lodging something seemed to question me: "What are the reasons that keep you from going to Rochester?" I could readily list them, but then the question returned: "Ah! but are these good reasons? Certainly you are needed at Rochester all the more because of these difficulties. Do you avoid the field because there are so many things that need to be corrected, because there is so much that is wrong? But if all was right, you would not be needed."

I soon came to the conclusion that we were all wrong, and that the reasons that had decided us against my going to Rochester were the most urgent reasons *for* my going. I felt ashamed to shrink from undertaking this work because of its difficulties, and it was strongly impressed upon me that the Lord would be with me and that was my field. So before I retired to rest my mind became entirely decided that Rochester was the place to which the Lord would have me go. I informed my wife of my decision, and accordingly, early in the morning, before the people were generally moving in the city, we left and went west on the canal boat instead of east. The brethren in Utica were greatly surprised when they learned of this change in our destination, and awaited the result with a good deal of concern.

Until I went to Rochester I had only in rare instances used as a means of promoting revivals what has since been called "the anxious seat." I had sometimes asked persons in the congregation to stand up, but this I had not done frequently. However, in studying the subject I had often felt the necessity of some measure that would bring sinners to a decision. From my own experience and observation I had found that the greatest obstacle to be overcome was their fear of being known as anxious inquirers. They were too proud to take any position that would reveal them to others as concerned for their souls.

I had found also that something was needed to make the impression on them that they were expected at once to give up their hearts; something that would call them to act, and act as publicly before the world as they had in their sins; something that would commit them publicly to the service of Christ. When I had called them simply to stand up in the public congregation, I found that this had a very good effect. So far as it went, it answered the purpose for which it was intended. But after all, I had felt for some time that something more was necessary to bring them out from among the mass of the ungodly to a public renunciation of their sinful ways and a public committal of themselves to God.

It was at Rochester that I first introduced this measure. This was years after the cry had been raised of "new measures." I made a call for the first time for persons who were willing to renounce their sins and give themselves to God to come forward to certain seats which I requested to be vacated, and offer themselves up to God while we made them subjects of prayer. A much larger number came forward than I expected.

I had always insisted much in my instructions upon entire consecration to God, giving up all to him—body, soul, possessions—to be forever after used for his glory as a condition of acceptance with God. Sinners were not encouraged to expect the Holy Spirit to convert them while they were passive, and never told to wait

God's time, but were taught unequivocally that their first and immediate duty was to submit themselves to God, to renounce their own will, their own way and themselves, and to instantly deliver up all that they were—and all that they had to their rightful owner, the Lord Jesus Christ. They were taught that the only obstacle in the way was their own stubborn will; that God was trying to gain their unqualified consent to give up their sins and accept the Lord Jesus Christ as their righteousness and salvation. The point was frequently urged upon them to give their consent and they were told that the only difficulty was to get their own honest and earnest consent to the terms upon which Christ would save them, and the lowest terms upon which they could possibly be saved.

Faith in God, and God in Christ, was ever made prominent. They were informed that this faith is not a mere intellectual assent, but is the consent or trust of the heart, a voluntary, intelligent trust in God as he is revealed in the Lord Jesus Christ. The doctrine of the justice of endless punishment was fully insisted upon, and not only its justice but the certainty that sinners will be endlessly punished if they die in their sins was strongly held forth.

Sinners were never taught, in any of the revivals, that they needed to expect conversion in answer to their own prayers. They were told that if they regarded iniquity in their hearts, the Lord would not hear them, and that while they remained impenitent they were sinning in their hearts, and that such impenitent and unbelieving prayer is an abomination to God. But if they were truly disposed to offer acceptable prayer to God they could do it, for there was nothing but their own obstinacy in the way of doing so at once. In short, pains were taken to shut the sinner up to accepting Christ—his whole will, atonement, official work and official relations, renouncing all sin, all excuse-making, all unbelief, all hardness of heart, and every wicked thing, in heart, and life, here, and now, forever.

On one occasion I had an appointment in another of the churches in the area. There had been a military parade in the city that day. The militia had been called out and I had feared that the excitement of the parade might divert the attention of the people and mar the work of the Lord, but the house was filled in every part. Dr. Penny had introduced the services and was engaged in the first prayer when I heard something which I supposed to be the report of a gun and the jingling of glass, as if a window had been broken. My thought was that some careless person from the military parade on the outside had fired so near the window as to break a pane of glass.

But before I had time to think again Dr. Penny leaped from the pulpit almost over me, for I was kneeling by the sofa behind him. The pulpit was in the front of the church, between the two doors. The rear wall of the church stood upon the brink of the canal. The congregation in a moment fell into a perfect panic and rushed for the doors and the windows in utter confusion. One elderly woman held up a window in the rear of the church, where several leaped out into the canal. The rush was terrific. Some jumped over the balcony rails into the aisles below running over each other.

I stood up in the pulpit, and not knowing what had happened put up my hands and cried at the top of my voice, "Be quiet! Be quiet!" Suddenly a couple of women rushing up into the pulpit, one on the one side and the other on the other side, caught hold of me in a state of panic. Dr. Penny ran out into the streets while some were getting out in every other direction as fast as possible.

Since I did not know there was any danger, the scene looked so ludicrous to me that I could scarcely refrain from laughing. They rushed over each other in the aisles and in several instances men who had been crushed down rose up and threw off others who had rushed upon them. All finally got out. Several were considerably hurt but no one killed. But the church was strewn with all sorts of women's apparel—bonnets, shawls, gloves, handkerchiefs and parts of dresses. The men had gone out without their hats and many persons had been seriously bruised in the awful rush.

Afterward I learned that the walls of the church had been settling for some time, the ground being very damp from its nearness to the canal. It had been spoken of in the congregation as not in a satisfactory state. Some were afraid that either the tower would fall, or the roof, or the walls of the building would come down. Of this I had heard nothing myself. The original alarm was created by a timber from the roof falling end downwards and breaking through the ceiling above the lamp in front of the organ.

On examining the building it was found that the walls had spread in such a manner that there was indeed danger of the roof falling in. The pressure that night in the balcony had been so great as to spread the walls on each side until there was real danger. At the time this occurred, I greatly feared that the public attention would be diverted and the work greatly hindered. But the Spirit of the Lord had taken hold of the work in earnest and nothing seemed to stop it. Another church was opened to us to continue the meetings.

I have not said much, as yet, of the spirit of prayer that prevailed in this revival, which I must not omit to mention. When I was on my way to Rochester, as we passed through a village some thirty miles east of Rochester, a brother minister whom I knew, seeing me in the canal-boat, jumped aboard to have a little conversation with me, intending to ride but a little way and return. He, however, became interested in conversation, and upon learning where I was going he made up his mind to go with me to Rochester.

We had been there but a few days when this minister became so convicted that he could not help weeping aloud, at one time, as he passed along the street. The Lord gave him a powerful spirit of prayer, and his heart was broken. As he and I prayed much together, I was struck by his faith in regard to what the Lord was going to do there. I remember he would say, "Lord, I do not know how it is, but I seem to know that thou art going to do a great work in this city." The spirit of prayer was poured out powerfully, so much so that some persons stayed away from the public service to pray, being unable to restrain their feelings under preaching.

And here I must introduce the name of a man whom I shall have occasion to mention frequently, Mr. Abel Clary. He was an elder of the church where I was converted. He was converted in the same revival in which I was. He had been licensed to preach, but the spirit of prayer made him so burdened for the souls of men that he was not able to preach much, his whole time and strength being given to prayer. The burden of his soul would frequently be so great that he was unable to stand and he would writhe and groan in agony. I was well acquainted with him and knew something of the wonderful spirit of prayer that was upon him. He was a very silent man, as almost all are who have that powerful spirit of prayer.

I learned of his being at Rochester from a gentleman who lived about a mile west of the city. He called me one day and asked me if I knew a Mr. Abel Clary, a minister. I told him that I knew him well. "Well," said he, "he is at my house, and has been there for some time, and I don't know what to think of him."

I said, "I have not seen him at any of our meetings."

"No," he replied, "he cannot go to meetings, he

says. He prays nearly all the time, day and night, and in such an agony of mind that I do not know what to make of it. Sometimes he cannot even stay on his knees, but will lie prostrate on the floor, and groan and pray in a manner that quite astonishes me."

I said to the brother, "I understand it; please keep still. It will all come out right; he will surely prevail."

I knew at the time a considerable number of men who were exercised in the same way. This Mr. Clary, and many others among the men and a large number of women, partook of the same spirit and spent a great part of their time in prayer. Father Nash, who in several of my fields of labor came to me and aided me, was another of those men that had such a powerful spirit of prevailing prayer. This Mr. Clary continued in Rochester as long as I did, and did not leave it until after I had left. He never appeared in public that I could learn, but gave himself wholly to prayer.

The moral aspect of things was greatly changed by this revival. It was a young city, full of thrift and enterprise, but also full of sin. The inhabitants were intelligent and enterprising in the highest degree, but as the revival swept through the town and converted the great mass of the most influential people, both men and women, the change in the order, sobriety, and morality of the city was wonderful.

The greatness of the work at Rochester at that time attracted so much of the attention of ministers and Christians throughout the state of New York, throughout New England, and in many parts of the United States, that the very fame of it was an efficient instrument in the hands of the Spirit of God in promoting the greatest revival throughout the land that this country had then ever witnessed.

Years after this, in conversing with Dr. Beecher about this powerful revival and its results, he remarked: "That was the greatest work of God, and the greatest revival that the world has ever seen in so short a time. One hundred thousand,'' he remarked, "were reported as having connected themselves with churches as the results of that great revival. This, is unparalleled in the history of the church." He spoke of this having been done within one year, and said that in no year during the Christian era had we any account of so great a revival in so short a time.

From the time of the convention which had opposed me, of which I have spoken, open and public opposition to revivals was less and less evident. Personally I met with much less opposition than I had before. It gradually but greatly subsided. At Rochester I felt nothing of it. Indeed the waters of salvation had risen so high, revivals had become so powerful and extensive, and people had had time to become acquainted with them and their results in such measure that men were afraid to oppose them. The conviction became nearly universal that they were the work of God.

21

During the latter part of the time that I was at Rochester my health was poor. I was worn out, and some of the leading physicians had made up their minds that I never would be able to preach anymore. My labors in Rochester at that time had continued through six months, and near their close Rev. Dr. Wisner of Ithaca came down and spent some time, witnessing and helping forward the work. In the meantime I was invited to many fields, among them to Union College at Schenectady to secure the conversion of the students. I made up my mind to comply with his request.

In company with Dr. Wisner I started in the stage in the spring of 1831 and the going was exceedingly bad. I left my wife and children for the time at Rochester as the travelling was too dangerous and the journey too fatiguing for them. When we arrived at Geneva Dr. Wisner insisted on my going home with him to rest a while. I declined and said I must keep about my work. He pressed me very hard to go and finally told me that the physicians in Rochester had told him to take me home with him, for I was going to die; that I would never labor anymore in revivals, for I had tuberculosis and would live but a little while. I replied that I had been told this before, but that it was a mistake. The doctors did not understand my case. I was only fatigued and a little rest would bring me up.

Dr. Wisner finally gave up pleading and I went on in the stage to Auburn. The going was so very bad that sometimes we could not get on more than two miles an hour, and we had been two or three days in going from Rochester to Auburn. As I had many dear friends in Auburn and was very much fatigued, I made up my mind to stop there and rest until the next stage came through. I had paid my fare through to Schenectady, but could stop over, if I chose, for one or more days. I stopped at the home of a very dear friend of mine.

In the morning, after sleeping quietly I had risen and was preparing to take the stage when a gentleman came in with the request for me to remain—a request in writing signed by that large number of influential men of whom I have spoken before as resisting the revival in that place in 1826. These men had carried their opposition so far as to break from Dr. Lansing's congregation and form a new one. The paper contained an earnest appeal to me to stop and labor for their salvation. This was very striking to me. In this paper they mentioned the opposition they had formerly made to my labors, begged me to overlook it, and stop and preach the Gospel to them.

This request did not come from the pastor, nor from his church, but from those who had formerly led the opposition to the work. The pastor and church members pressed me to remain and comply with the request of these men. They appeared as much surprised as I at the change in the attitude of those men. I went to my room and spread the subject before God, and soon made up my mind what to do. I told the pastor and his elders that I was very much worn out, but that upon certain conditions I would remain. I would preach twice on Sundays and two evenings during the week, but they should take all the rest of the labor upon themselves, instructing inquirers, conducting the prayer and other meetings, and not expect me to attend any other meetings than those at which I preached. I furthermore stipulated that neither they nor their people should visit me at my lodgings except in extreme cases, that I might rest.

The word took immediate effect. On the first or second Sunday evening that I preached I saw that the word was taking such powerful hold that at the close I called for those whose minds were made up to come forward, publicly renounce their sins, and give themselves to Christ. Much to my own surprise, and very much to the surprise of the pastor and many members of the church, the first man whom I observed coming forward was the man who had led the opposition to the former revival. He was followed by a large number of the persons who had signed that paper.

I have spoken of Mr. Clary as the praying man who was at Rochester. He had a brother, a physician, living in Auburn. I think it was the second Sunday that I was at Auburn that I observed in the congregation the solemn face of this Mr. Clary. He looked as if he was borne down with an agony of prayer. Being well acquainted with him, and knowing the great gift of God that was upon him, the spirit of prayer, I was very glad to see him there. He sat in the pew with his brother, the doctor, who was also a professing Christian but had never experienced his brother Abel's great power with God.

At noon, as soon as I came down from the pulpit Mr. Clary, with his brother, met me at the pulpit stairs, and the doctor invited me to go home with him for dinner. I did so.

After arriving at his house we were soon summoned to the dinner table. We gathered about the table, and Dr. Clary turned to his brother and said, "Brother Abel, will you ask a blessing?"

Brother Abel bowed his head and began, audibly, to ask a blessing. He had uttered but a sentence or two when he instantly broke down, moved suddenly back from the table, and fled to his room.

The doctor supposed he had been taken suddenly ill, and rose up and followed him. In a few moments he came down and said, "Mr. Finney, brother Abel wants to see you."

"What ails him?"

"I do not know, but he says you know. He appears in great distress, but I think it is a state of mind."

I understood it in a moment, and went to his room. He lay groaning upon the bed, the Spirit making intercession for him, and in him, with groanings that could not be uttered.

I had barely entered the room when he made out to say, "Pray, brother Finney."

I knelt down and helped him in prayer by leading his soul out for the conversion of sinners. I continued to pray until his distress passed away, and then I returned to the dinner table.

I understood that this was the voice of God. I saw the spirit of prayer was upon him, and I felt his influence upon myself and took it for granted that the work would move on powerfully. It did so.

After Dr. Wisner returned to Boston I soon received a request from the Congregational ministers and churches to go to that city and labor. I began my labors there by preaching around in the different churches on Sundays, and on week evenings I preached in Park Street. I perceived that there needed to be a great searching among professed Christians. I could not learn that there was among them anything like the spirit of prayer that had prevailed in the revivals in the West and in New York City. There seemed to be a peculiar type of religion there, not exhibiting that freedom and strength of faith which I had been in the habit of seeing in New York.

I therefore began to preach some searching sermons

to Christians. I soon found that these sermons were
not at all palatable to the Christians of Boston. It was
something they never had been used to, and the attendance at Park Street became less and less, especially
on those evenings when I preached to professed Christians. This was new to me. I had never before seen
professed Christians shrink back, as they did at that
time in Boston, from searching sermons. It was evident
that they resented my plain dealing and that my searching sermons astonished and even offended very many
of them. However, as the work went forward this state
of things changed greatly. After a few weeks they would
listen to searching preaching and came to appreciate
it.

Some earnest brethren wrote to me from New York
about this time, proposing to lease a theater and fit
it up for a church, upon condition that I would come
there and preach. They proposed to get the Chatham
Street theater, in the heart of the most irreligious population of New York. It was owned by men who were
very willing to have it transformed into a church. At
this time we had three children, and I could not well
take my family with me while laboring as an evangelist.
My strength, too, had become a good deal exhausted.
On praying and looking the matter over, I concluded
that I would accept the call and labor, for a time
at least, in New York.

22

I left Boston in April, 1832, and began labors in the theater in New York. The Spirit of the Lord was immediately poured out upon us, and we had an extensive revival that spring and summer.

About midsummer cholera appeared in New York for the first time. The panic became great and a great many Christian people fled into the country. Cholera was very severe in the city that summer, more so than it ever has been since and it was especially fatal in the part of the city where I resided. I remember counting, from the door of our house, five hearses drawn up at the same time at different doors within sight. I remained in New York until the latter part of the summer, not willing to leave the city while the mortality was so great. But I found that the influence was undermining my health, and in the latter part of the summer I went into the country for two or three weeks. On my return I was installed as pastor of the Chatham Street Chapel.

During the installation services I was taken ill, and soon after I got home it was plain that I was seized with cholera. The gentleman next door took ill about the same time and before morning he was dead. The means used for my recovery gave my system a terrible shock, from which it took me long to recover. However, toward spring I was able to preach again. I invited two ministerial brethren to help me in holding a series of meetings. We preached in turn for two or three weeks, but very little was accomplished. I saw that it was not the way to promote a revival there, and drew the meetings, in that form, to a close.

On the next Sunday I made appointments to preach every evening during the week, and a revival began immediately and became very powerful. My health was not yet vigorous, and after preaching twenty evenings in succession, I suspended that form of my labors. The converts known to us numbered five hundred, and our church became so large that very soon a group of believers was sent off to form another church.

The work continued to go forward in a very interesting manner. We held meetings of inquiry once or twice a week, and sometimes more often, and found that every week a goodly number of conversions were reported. The church members were praying, working people. They would go out into the highways and hedges and bring people to hear preaching whenever they were called upon to do so. Both men and women would undertake this work. When we wished to give notice of any extra meetings, little slips of paper, on which was printed an invitation to attend the services, would be carried from house to house in every direction by the members of the church. Thus the church could be filled any evening of the week. Our ladies were not afraid to go and gather in all classes of society from the neighborhood round about. It was something new to have religious services in that theater rather than such scenes as had formerly been enacted there.

There were three rooms connected with the front part of the theater, long, large rooms, which we fitted up for prayer meetings and for a lecture room. I instructed my church members to scatter themselves over the whole house and to keep their eyes open, in regard to any that were seriously affected under preaching, and if possible to detain them after preaching for conversation and prayer. They were true to their teaching and were on the lookout at every meeting to see with whom the Word of God was taking effect. They had faith enough to dismiss their fears and to speak to any whom they saw to be affected by the Word. In this way the conversion of a great many souls was secured. They would invite them into those rooms, and there we could converse and pray with them.

When I first went to Chatham Street Chapel, I informed the brethren that I did not wish to fill up the house with Christians from other churches, as my object was to gather from the world. I wanted to secure the conversion of the ungodly to the utmost possible extent. We therefore gave ourselves to labor for that class of persons, and by the blessing of God, with good success. Conversions were multiplied so much that our church soon became so large that we sent off another group of believers to form a church. When I left New York we had seven churches thus begun, whose members were laboring with all their might to secure the salvation of souls.

When I first went to New York I had made up my mind on the question of slavery and was exceedingly anxious to arouse public attention to the subject. I did not turn aside to make it a hobby or divert the attention of the people from the work of converting souls. But in my prayers and preaching I so often referred to slavery and denounced it that a considerable excitement came to exist among the people.

In January, 1834, I was obliged to leave on account of my health and take a sea voyage. I went up the Mediterranean in a small brig in the midst of winter. We had a very stormy passage. My stateroom was small, and I was, on the whole, very uncomfortable. The voyage did not much improve my health. I spent some weeks at Malta and also in Sicily. I was gone about six months. On my return I found that there was a great excitement in New York. The members of my church, together with others opposed to slavery in New York, had held a meeting on the Fourth of July and had had an address on the subject of slaveholding. A mob was stirred up, and this was the beginning of that series of mobs that spread in many directions, whenever and wherever there was an anti-slavery gathering, or a voice lifted up against the abominable institution of slavery.

However, I went forward in my labors in Chatham Street. The church continued to flourish and to extend its influence and its labors in every direction until the tabernacle in Broadway was completed. However, when the tabernacle was in the process of completion, its walls being up and the roof on, a story was circulated that it was going to be "an integrated church" in which black and white people were to be compelled to sit together throughout the sanctuary. Such was the state of the public mind in New York at that time that somebody set the building on fire. The firemen also were in such a state of mind that they refused to put it out and left the interior and roof to be consumed. However, the gentlemen who had undertaken to build it went ahead and completed it after the fire.

As the excitement increased on the subject of slavery, Mr. Leavitt espoused the cause of the slave, and advocated it in the little paper we had begun to distribute called the New York *Evangelist*. I was about to leave on the sea voyage to which I have referred, and cautioned Mr. Leavitt not to go too fast in the discussion of the anti-slavery question, lest he destroy his paper.

On my homeward passage my mind became exceedingly exercised on the question of revivals. I feared that they would decline throughout the country. I feared that the opposition that had been made to them had grieved the Holy Spirit. My own health seemed to have quite broken down, and I knew of no other evangelist that would take the field and aid pastors in revival work.

This view of the subject distressed me so much that one day I found myself unable to rest. My soul was in an utter agony. I spent almost the entire day in prayer in my stateroom or walking the deck in intense agony, in view of the state of things. In fact, I felt crushed with the burden that was on my soul. There was no one on board to whom I could open my mind or say a word.

It was the spirit of prayer that was upon me, that which I had often before experienced in kind but perhaps never before to such a degree, for so long a time. I besought the Lord to go on with his work and to provide himself with such instrumentalities as were necessary. It was a long summer day in the early part of July. After a day of unspeakable wrestling and agony in my soul, just at night the subject cleared up in my mind. The Spirit led me to believe that all would come out all right and that God had yet a work for me to do. I could be at rest, for the Lord would go forward with his work and give me strength to take any part in it that he desired. But I had no idea what course his providence would be.

On arriving at New York I found, as I have said, the mob excitement on the subject of slavery very intense. Mr. Leavitt came to me and said, "Brother Finney, I have ruined the *Evangelist*. My subscription list is rapidly failing, and we shall not be able to continue its publication past January unless you can do something to bring the paper back into public favor again."

I told him my health was such that I did not know what I could do, but I would make it a subject of prayer. After considering a day or two, I proposed to preach a course of lectures to my people on revivals which he might report for his paper.

He caught this at once and said, "That is the very thing." This had the effect he desired, and the subscription list rapidly increased.

I did not myself write the lectures, of course; they were wholly extemporaneous. Brother Leavitt's reports were meager, as it respects the matter contained in the lectures. The lectures averaged not less than an hour and three quarters in their delivery. But all that he could catch and report could be read in about thirty minutes.

These lectures were later published in a book called *Finney's Lectures on Revivals.* Twelve thousand copies were sold, as fast as they could be printed. And here, for the glory of Christ, I must add that they have been reprinted in England and France, translated into Welsh, French and German, and were very extensively circulated throughout Europe and the colonies of Great Britain.

After they had been printed in Welsh, the Congregational ministers of the Principality of Wales appointed a committee to inform me of the great revival that had resulted from the translation of those lectures into the Welsh language. This they did by letter. These revival lectures, meager as was the report of them, and feeble as they were themselves, have been instrumental in promoting revivals in England and Scotland as well as Wales, on the continent of Europe, in Canada East and West, in Nova Scotia and in some of the islands of the sea.

In England and Scotland I have often been refreshed by meeting with ministers and laymen in great numbers who had been converted, directly or indirectly, through the instrumentality of those lectures. When they were first published in the New York *Evangelist,* the reading of them resulted in revivals in multitudes of places throughout the United States also.

But this was not of man's wisdom. Let the reader remember that long day of agony and prayer at sea, that God would do something to forward the work of revivals, and enable me, if he desired to do it, to take such a course as to help forward the work. I felt certain then that my prayers would be answered; and I have regarded all that I have since been able to accomplish as an answer to the prayers of that day. The spirit of prayer came upon me as a sovereign grace, bestowed upon me without the least merit and in spite of all my sinfulness. He pressed my soul in prayer until I was able to prevail. Through the infinite riches of grace in Christ Jesus I have for many years witnessed the wonderful results of that day of wrestling with God. In answer to that day's agony, he has continued to give me the spirit of prayer.

23

Soon after I returned to New York I began my labors in the new tabernacle. The Spirit of the Lord was poured out upon us and we had a precious revival as long as I continued to be pastor of that church. While in New York I had many applications from young men to take them as students in theology. The number of applications became so large that I made up my mind to deliver a course of theological lectures in one of the larger rooms, and let such students as chose attend them without fee.

But before I had opened my lectures, in January 1835, Rev. John Jay Shipherd of Oberlin and a companion arrived in New York to persuade me to go to Oberlin as professor of theology. Mr. Shipherd had founded a church and organized a school at Oberlin about a year before this time and had obtained a charter broad enough for a university.

I said to Mr. Shipherd that I would not go unless two points were conceded by the trustees. One was that they should never interfere with the internal regulation of the school, but should leave that entirely to the discretion of the faculty. The other was that we should be allowed to receive black people on the same conditions that we did white people, that there should be no discrimination made on account of color.

When these conditions were forwarded to Oberlin

the trustees were called together, and after a great struggle to overcome their own prejudices and the prejudices of the community, they passed resolutions complying with the conditions proposed. This difficulty being removed, the friends in New York were called together to see what they could do about endowing the institution.

But still there was a great difficulty in leaving my church in New York. I had never thought of having my labors at Oberlin interfere with my revival labors and preaching. It was therefore agreed between myself and the church that I should spend my winters in New York and my summers in Oberlin, and that the church would be at the expense of my going and coming. When this was arranged I took my family and arrived in Oberlin at the beginning of summer, 1835.

The trustees put up "barracks" for housing, and students thronged to us from every direction. After I was engaged to come, the brethren at Oberlin wrote requesting me to bring a large tent to hold meetings in, as there was no room in the place large enough to accommodate the people. I made this request known to some of my brethren, who told me to go and get a tent made and they would furnish the money. This tent was of great service to us. When the weather would permit we spread it upon the town square every Sunday and held public services in it, and several of our earliest graduations were held in it. It was used to some extent also for holding extended meetings in the region round about, where there were no churches large enough to meet the necessities.

We had just barely entered upon the work of putting up our buildings and had arranged for a large amount of money, when the great commercial crash prostrated our leading contributor and nearly all the men who had subscribed for the fund for the support of the faculty. The commercial crash went over the country and prostrated the great mass of wealthy men. It left us not only without funds for the support of the faculty, but also thirty thousand dollars in debt, without any prospect that we could see of obtaining funds from the friends of the college in this country.

The great mass of people of Ohio were utterly opposed to our enterprise because of its anti-slavery character. The towns around us were hostile to our movement, and in some places threats were made to tear down our buildings. A democratic legislature was, in the meantime, endeavoring to get some hold of us that would enable them to withdraw our charter. In this dilemma there was, of course, a great crying to God among the people here.

In the meantime, my revival lectures had been very extensively circulated in England and we were aware that the British public would strongly sympathize with us if they knew our objectives and our condition. We therefore sent an agency to England, having obtained for them letters of recommendation from some of the leading anti-slavery men of the country. The British public generously responded and gave us six thousand pounds sterling. This very nearly cancelled our indebtedness.

Our friends scattered throughout the northern states, who were opposed to slavery and friends of revivals, generously aided us to the extent of their ability. But we had to struggle with poverty and many trials for years. Sometimes we did not know from day to day how we were to be provided for. But with the blessing of God we continued on as best we could.

At one time I saw no means of providing for my family through the winter. Thanksgiving day came and found us so poor that I was obliged to sell my travelling trunk, which I had used in my evangelistic labors, to replace a cow which I had lost. I rose on the morning of Thanksgiving and spread our necessities before the

Lord. I finally concluded by saying that if help did not come, I would assume that it was best that it should not, and would be entirely satisfied with any course that the Lord would see it wise to take. I went and preached, and enjoyed my own preaching as well as I ever did. I had a blessed day to my own soul, and I could see that the people enjoyed it exceedingly.

After the meeting I was detained a little while in conversation with some brethren and my wife returned home. When I reached the gate she was standing in the open door with a letter in her hand. As I approached she smilingly said, "The answer has come, my dear," and handed me the letter containing a check for two hundred dollars from Mr. Josiah Chapin of Providence.

He had been here the previous summer with his wife. I had said nothing about my wants at all, as I never was in the habit of mentioning them to anybody. But in the letter containing the check, he said he had learned that the endowment fund had failed and that I was in want of help. He intimated that I might expect more from time to time. He continued to send me six hundred dollars a year for several years, and on this I managed to live.

I spent my summers at Oberlin and my winters in New York for two or three years. We had a blessed reviving whenever I returned to preach there. We also had a revival at Oberlin continually. Very few students came without being converted.

During the summer months there was a great pressure upon the people at Oberlin. The students engaged in preparing for the anniversaries of their various college societies, for their examinations, and for graduation. Of course during the summer term there was a great deal of excitement unfavorable to the progress of a revival. We had much more of this excitement in later years than we had at first. College societies have increased in number and other interesting occasions have been multiplied so that it has become more and more difficult to secure a powerful revival during the summer term. This ought not to be.

I began to see that an impression seemed to be growing in Oberlin that during term time we could not expect to have a revival, and that our revivals must be expected to occur during the long vacations in the winter. This was not deliberately decided by anyone, and yet it was plain that that was coming to be the impression. But I had come to Oberlin and resided here for the sake of securing the conversion and sanctification of the students. It was only because there was so great a number of them there, which gave me such a good opportunity to work on so many young minds in the process of education, that I had remained there from year to year. Frequently I had almost made up my mind to leave and give myself wholly to the work of an evangelist. But the plea always was that we could not do as much in this country in promoting revivals anywhere, except during the long vacation. I could do more good at Oberlin during term time—that is, in the spring, summer, and early autumn—than I could anywhere else.

Our fall term was properly our harvest here. It began about the first of September when he had a large number of new students, and many of these were unconverted. I always felt, as a good many others had, that during that term was the time to secure the conversion of our new students. Our revival efforts took effect among the students from year to year because they were aimed at securing the conversion especially of the students. Our general population was a changing one, and we very frequently needed a sweeping revival through the whole town, among the householders as well as the students, to keep up a healthy tone of piety.

A goodly number of our students had learned to

work in promoting revivals and were very efficient in laboring for the conversion of their fellow students. The young men's prayer meetings were also blessed. The efforts of brothers and sisters in the church had been increasingly blessed from year to year. We had more or less a continual revival, summer and winter.

24

My health soon became such that I found I must relinquish one of my fields of labor. The interests connected with the college seemed to forbid utterly that I should leave it, so I took a dismission from my church in New York. The winter months which I was to have spent in New York I spent in laboring in various places to promote revivals.

The two winters before leaving New York, after my lectures on revivals, I gave lectures to Christians, which were also reported by Mr. Leavitt in the New York *Evangelist*. Those sermons to Christians were very much the result of a searching that was going on in my own mind. I mean that the Spirit of God was showing me many things in regard to the question of sanctification that led me to preach those sermons to Christians.

Many Christians regarded those lectures as an exhibition of the Law rather than of the Gospel. But I did not, and do not, so regard them. For me the Law and Gospel have but one rule of life, and every violation of the spirit of the Law is also a violation of the spirit of the Gospel. I have long been satisfied that the higher forms of Christian experience are attained only as a result of a terribly searching application of God's law to the human conscience and heart. The result of my labors up to that time had shown me more clearly than I had known before the great weakness of Christians, and that the older members of the church, as a general thing, were making very little progress in grace. I found that they would fall back from a revival state even sooner than young converts. It had been so in the revival in which I myself was converted. I saw clearly that this was due to their early teaching; that is, to the views which they had been led to entertain when they were young converts.

I was also led into a state of great dissatisfaction with my own lack of stability in faith and love. To be candid and tell the truth, I must say, to the praise of God's grace, he did not allow me to backslide to the extent many Christians did. But I often felt myself weak in the presence of temptation, and needed frequently to hold days of fasting and prayer, and to spend much time in overhauling my own religious life in order to retain that communion with God and that hold upon the divine strength that would enable me to labor efficiently for the promotion of revivals.

In looking at the state of the Christian church as it had been revealed to me in my revival labors, I was led earnestly to inquire whether there was something higher and more enduring that the Christian church was aware of; whether there were promises and means provided in the Gospel for the establishment of Christians in altogether a higher form of Christian life. I had known somewhat of the view of sanctification entertained by our Methodist brethren. But as their idea of sanctification seemed to me to relate almost completely to states of emotional feeling, I could not receive their teaching. However, I gave myself earnestly to search the Scriptures and to read whatever came to hand upon the subject until my mind was satisfied that an altogether higher and more stable form of Christian life was attainable and was the privilege of all Christians. This led me to preach two sermons on

Christian perfection in the Broadway Tabernacle.

But about this time the question of Christian perfection in the antinomian sense of the term came to be agitated a good deal in the East. I examined these views, as published in the periodical entitled *The Perfectionist*, but I could not accept them. Yet I was satisfied that the doctrine of sanctification in this life, and entire santification, in the sense that it was the privilege of Christians to live without known sin, was a doctrine taught in the Bible and that abundant means were provided for the securing of that attainment.

The last winter that I spent in New York the Lord was pleased to visit my soul with a great refreshing. After a season of great searching of heart he brought me, as he has often done, into a large place and gave me much of that divine sweetness in my soul of which Jonathan Edwards speaks as attained in his own experience. That winter I had a thorough breaking up—so much so that sometimes for a considerable period I could not refrain from loud weeping in view of my own sins and of the love of God in Christ. Such seasons were frequent that winter and resulted in the great renewal of my spiritual strength and enlargement of my views in regard to the privileges of Christians and the abundance of the grace of God.

But after I came to Oberlin, within a year or two the cry of antinomian perfectionism was heard, and this charge was brought against us. Letters were written, ecclesiastical bodies were visited, and many pains were taken throughout the length and breadth of the land to represent our views as entirely heretical. This led to many ecclesiastical bodies passing resolutions warning the churches against the influence of Oberlin theology. There seemed to be a general union of ministerial influence against us. But we said nothing. We had no controversy with those brethren who were taking pains to raise such a powerful public sentiment against us. We kept about our own business and felt that in respect to opposition from that quarter, our strength was to sit still, and we were not mistaken. We felt confident that it was not God's plan to allow such opposition to prevail. The policy that we pursued was to let opposition alone. We kept about our own business and always had as many students as we knew what to do with. Our hands were always full of labor, and we were always greatly encouraged in our efforts.

One of the leading ministers who had heard much of the opposition spent a day or two at our house. He said to me: "Brother Finney, Oberlin is to us a great wonder. The ministers almost universally arrayed themselves against Oberlin, and many denominations have warned their churches against you and discouraged young men from coming to Oberlin, and still the Lord has built you up. You are supported with funds better than almost any college in the West; you have had far more students, and the blessing of God has been upon you so that your success has been wonderful. The opposers of Oberlin have been confounded. God has stood by you and sustained you through all this opposition, so that you have hardly felt it."

It is difficult now for people to realize the opposition we met with when we first established this college. An illustration of it, a representative case, occurred when I had occasion to go to Akron to preach one Sunday. I went with a horse and carriage. On my way I observed in the road before me a woman walking with a little bundle in her hand. As I drew near her, I observed that she was an elderly woman, nicely dressed, but walking with some difficulty on account of her age. As I came up to her I reined up my horse and asked her how far she was going on that road. She told me, and I then asked if she would accept a ride in my carriage.

"Oh," she replied, "I would be very thankful for

a ride, for I find I have undertaken too long a walk." I helped her in and drove on. I found her a very intelligent lady, free and homelike in her conversation.

After riding for some distance she said, "May I ask to whom I am indebted for this ride?" I told her who I was. She then inquired from whence I came. I told her I was from Oberlin.

This announcement startled her. She made a motion as if she would sit as far from me as she could, and turning and looking earnestly at me she said, "From Oberlin! why," she said, "our minister said he would just as soon send a son to state prison as to Oberlin!" Of course I smiled and soothed the old lady's fears, and made her understand she was in no danger from me.

During these years of smoke and dust, of misapprehension and opposition from without, the Lord was blessing us richly within. We not only prospered in our own souls there as a church, but we had a continuous revival, or were in what might properly be regarded as a revival state. Our students were converted by scores and the Lord overshadowed us continually with the cloud of his mercy. Gales of divine influence swept over us from year to year, producing abundantly the fruits of the Spirit—"love, joy, peace, longsuffering, gentleness, goodness, faith, meekness, temperance."

I have always attributed our success in this good work entirely to the grace of God. It was no wisdom or goodness of our own that achieved this success. Nothing but continued divine influence pervading the community sustained us under our trials and kept us in an attitude of mind in which we could be efficient in the work we had undertaken. We have always felt that if the Lord withheld his Spirit, no outward circumstances could make us truly prosperous.

When the question of entire sanctification first

came up here for public discussion, and when the subject first attracted the general attention of the church, we were in the midst of a powerful revival. The point that I pressed upon the people was the distinction between desire and will, so that they might know whether they were really Christians or not, whether they were really consecrated persons, or whether they merely had desires without being in fact willing to obey God.

When this distinction was made clear the Holy Spirit fell upon the congregation in a most remarkable manner. A large number of persons dropped down their heads and some groaned so that they could be heard throughout the house. It cut up the false hopes of deceived professing Christians on every side. Several rose on the spot and said that they had been deceived and that they could see where. This was carried to such an extent as greatly astonished me; indeed, it produced a general feeling of astonishment in the congregation.

The work went on with power, professing Christians obtaining new hope, or being genuinely converted in such numbers that a very great and important change came over the whole community. In a few days after this, one of our theological students rose and asked whether the Gospel provided for Christians all the conditions of an established faith, and hope, and love; whether there was something better and higher than Christians had generally experienced; in short, whether sanctification was attainable in this life; that is, sanctification in such a sense that Christians could have unbroken peace, and not come into condemnation or have the feeling of condemnation or a consciousness of sin.

The president of the school immediately answered, "Yes." What occurred at this meeting brought the question of sanctification prominently before us as a practical question. We had no theories on the subject, no philosophy to maintain, but simply took it up as a Bible question. In this form it existed among us as an experimental truth, which we did not attempt to reduce to a theological formula until years afterward. The discussion of the question was a great blessing to us and to a great number of our students.

25

In the fall of 1843 I was called again to Boston. At my last visit there it was the time of the greatest excitement in Boston, on the subject of the second advent of Christ. Mr. Miller, who was at the head of the movement, was there lecturing, and was holding daily Bible classes in which he was giving instruction and teaching his peculiar views. His teaching led to intense excitement involving much that was wild and irrational. I attended Mr. Miller's Bible class once or twice, after which I invited him to my room and tried to convince him that he was in error. The last time that I had attended his Bible class he was teaching the doctrine that Christ would come personally and destroy his enemies in 1843.

When I arrived there in the fall of 1843 I found that that particular form of excitement had blown over, but many forms of error prevailed among the people, much as when I had first labored there. I was told at that time, "Mr. Finney, you cannot labor here as you do elsewhere. You have got to begin at the foundation, for Unitarianism is strong here. It is a system of denials, and under its teaching the foundations of Christianity are falling away. The Unitarians and the Universalists, who teach that everybody will be saved, have destroyed the foundations, and the people are all afloat. Almost any conceivable form of error may get a hearing and find followers."

I have since found this to be true, to a greater extent than in any other field in which I have ever labored. The mass of the people in Boston are more unsettled in their religious convictions than in any other place that I have ever labored in, notwithstanding their intelligence. It is extremely difficult to make religious truths lodge in their minds, because the influence of Unitarian teaching has been to lead them to call in question all the principle doctrines of the Bible, denying the reality of the Trinity and the deity of Christ. Their system is one of denials. Their theology is negative. They deny almost everything, and affirm almost nothing. In such a field error finds the ears of the people open.

I have labored in Boston in five powerful revivals. I must express it as my sincere conviction that the greatest difficulty in the way of overcoming Unitarianism, and all the forms of error there, is the timidity of Christians and churches. The orthodox churches there are too formal. They are in bondage to certain ways. They are afraid of doing things in new ways, afraid to launch forth in all freedom in the use of means to save souls. The ministers and deacons of the churches, though good men, are afraid to wake up the people. They think everything must be done in a certain way. The Holy Spirit is grieved by their yielding to such bondage.

I began my labors in the Marlborough chapel at this time and found there a very singular state of things. A church had been formed composed greatly of radicals, and most of the members held extreme views on various subjects. They had come out from other orthodox churches and united in a church of their own at Marlborough chapel. They were staunch, and many of them consistent reformers. They were good people, but I cannot say that they were a united people.

Their extreme views seemed to be an element of mutual repellance among them. Some of them were extreme nonresistants and held it to be wrong to use any physical force, or any physical means whatever, even in controlling their own children. Everything must be done by moral persuasion. Upon the whole, however, they were a praying, earnest, Christian people. I found no particular difficulty in getting along with them; but at that time the Miller excitement and various other causes had been operating to cause a good deal of confusion among them. They were not at all in a prosperous state, as a church.

A young man had risen up among them who professed to be a prophet. I had many conversations with him and tried to convince him that he was wrong, and I labored with his followers to try to make them see that he was wrong. However, I found it impossible to do anything with him or with them until he finally committed himself on several points and predicted that certain things would happen at certain dates. One was that his father would die on a certain day.

I then said to him: "Now we shall prove you. If these things that you predict come to pass, and come to pass at certain times, as you say they will, then we shall have reason to believe that you are a prophet. But if they do not come to pass, it will prove that you are deceived."

This he could not deny. He had staked his reputation as a prophet upon the truth of these predictions, and awaited their fulfillment. Of course every one of them failed, and he failed with them. I never heard anything more of his predictions. But he had confused a good many minds and really neutralized their efforts, and I am not aware that those who were his followers ever regained their former influence as Christians.

During this winter the Lord gave my own soul a very thorough overhauling and a fresh baptism of his

Spirit. I boarded at the Marlborough hotel, and my study and bedroom were in one corner of the chapel building. My mind was greatly drawn out in prayer for a long time, as indeed it always has been when I have labored in Boston. I have been favored there, uniformly, with a great deal of the spirit of prayer. But this winter in particular my mind was exceedingly exercised on the question of personal holiness; and in respect to the state of the church, their lack of power with God; the weakness of the orthodox churches in Boston, the weakness of their faith, and their lack of power in the midst of such a community. The fact that they were making little or no progress in overcoming the errors of that city greatly affected my mind.

I gave myself to a great deal of prayer. After my evening services I would retire as early as I could, but rose at four o'clock in the morning because I could sleep no longer, and immediately went to the study and engaged in prayer. And so deeply was my mind exercised, and so absorbed in prayer, that I frequently continued from the time I arose, at four o'clock, until the gong called to breakfast at eight o'clock.

My days were spent, so far as I could get time, in searching the Scriptures. I read nothing else, all that winter, but my Bible; and a great deal of it seemed new to me. Again the Lord took me, as it were, from Genesis to Revelation. He led me to see the connection of things, the promises, threatenings, the prophecies and their fulfillment; and indeed, the whole Scripture seemed to me all ablaze with light, and not only light, but it seemed as if God's Word was vibrant with the very life of God.

After praying in this way for weeks and months, one morning while I was engaged in prayer the thought occurred to me: What if, after all this divine teaching, my will is not carried, and this teaching takes effect only in my feelings of intellectual pleasure? May it not be that my emotions are affected by these revelations from reading the Bible, and my heart is not really subdued by them? At this point several passages of scripture occurred to me, such as this: "Line must be upon line, precept upon precept, precept upon precept, here a little, and there a little, that they might go and fall backward, and be snared and taken."

The thought that I might be deceiving myself, when it first occurred to me, stung me almost like an adder. It created a pang that I cannot describe. The passages of scripture that occurred to me in that direction, for a few moments greatly increased my distress. But soon I was enabled to fall back upon the perfect will of God. I said to the Lord that if he saw it was wise and best, and that his honor demanded that I should be left to be deluded and go down to hell, I accepted his will and I said to him, "Do with me as seems good to thee."

Just before this occurrence I had a great struggle to consecrate myself to God in a higher sense than I had ever before seen to be my duty, or conceived as possible. I had often before laid my family upon the altar of God, and left them to be disposed of at his discretion. But at this time that I now speak of, I had had a great struggle about giving up my wife to the will of God. She was in very feeble health, and it was evident that she could not live long. I had never before seen so clearly what was implied in laying her and all that I possessed upon the altar of God, and for hours I struggled upon my knees to give her up unqualifiedly to the will of God. I found myself unable to do it. I was so shocked and surprised at this that I perspired profusely with agony. I struggled and prayed until I was exhausted, and found myself entirely unable to give her altogether up to God's will, in such a way as to make no objection to his disposing of her just as he pleased.

This troubled me much. I wrote to my wife, telling her what a struggle I had had and the concern that I had felt at not being willing to commit her without reserve to the perfect will of God. This was but a very short time before I had this temptation of which I have spoken, when those passages of scripture came so distressingly to my mind, and when the bitterness, almost of death, seemed for a few moments to possess me at the thought that my religion might be of my mind and emotions only, and that God's teaching might have taken effect only in my feelings. But as I said, I was enabled after struggling for a few moments with this discouragement and bitterness, which I have since attributed to a fiery dart of Satan, to fall back in a deeper sense than I had ever done before upon the infinitely blessed and perfect will of God. I then told the Lord that I had such confidence in him that I felt perfectly willing to give myself, my wife and my family all to be disposed of according to his own wisdom.

I then had a deeper view than ever before of what was implied in consecration to God. I spent a long time upon my knees in considering the matter all over again and giving up everything to the will of God— the interests of the church, the progress of religion, the conversion of the world, and the salvation or damnation of my own soul, as the will of God might decide. Indeed, I remember that I went so far as to say to the Lord with all my heart that he might do anything with me or mine to which his blessed will could consent; that I had such perfect confidence in his goodness and love as to believe he could consent to do nothing to which I could object. I felt a kind of holy boldness in telling him to do with me just as seemed good to him; that he could not do anything that was not perfectly wise and good; therefore I had the best of grounds for accepting whatever he could consent to in respect to me and mine. So deep and perfect a resting in the will of God I had never known before.

What has appeared strange to me is this, that I could not get hold of my former hope, nor could I remember, with any freshness, any of the former seasons of communion and divine assurances that I had experienced. I may say that I gave up my hope and rested everything upon a new foundation. I mean, I gave up hope from any past experience, and remember telling the Lord that I did not know whether he intended to save me or not. Nor did I feel concerned to know. I said that if I found that he kept me and worked in me by his Spirit and was preparing me for heaven, working holiness and eternal life in my soul, I would take it for granted that he intended to save me. If, on the other hand, I found myself empty of divine strength and light and love, I would conclude that he saw it wise and expedient to send me to hell, and that in either event I would accept his will. My mind settled to a perfect stillness.

This was early in the morning, and through the whole of that day I seemed to be in a state of perfect rest—body and soul. The question frequently arose in my mind during the day, "Do you still hold to your consecration and abide in the will of God?"

I said without hesitation, "Yes, I take nothing back. I have no reason for taking anything back. I do not want to take anything back." The thought that I might be lost did not distress me. Indeed, think as I might, during that whole day I could not find in my mind the least fear, the least disturbing emotion. Nothing troubled me. I was neither elated nor depressed. I was neither joyful nor sorrowful. My confidence in God was perfect, my acceptance of his will was perfect, and my mind was as calm as heaven.

Just at evening the question arose in my mind, "What if God should send me to hell, what then?"

"Why, I would not object to it."

"But can he send a person to hell who accepts his will, in the sense in which you do?"

This inquiry was no sooner raised in my mind than settled. I said, "No, it is impossible. Hell could be no hell to me if I accepted God's perfect will."

This sprung a vein of joy in my mind that kept developing more and more, for weeks and months, and indeed I may say, for years. For years my mind was too full of joy to feel much exercised with anxiety on any subject. My prayer that had been so fervent, and protracted during so long a period, seemed all to run out into, "Thy will be done." It seemed as if my desires were all met. What I had been praying for, for myself, I had received in a way that I least expected. Holiness to the Lord seemed to be inscribed on all the exercises of my mind. I had such strong faith that God would accomplish all his perfect will that I could not be anxious about anything. The great anxieties about which my mind had been exercised during my seasons of agonizing prayer seemed to be set aside, so that for a long time when I went to God to commune with him, as I did very, very frequently, I would fall on my knees and find it impossible to ask for anything with any earnestness except that his will might be done in earth as it is done in heaven. My prayers were swallowed up in that, and I often found myself smiling, as it were, in the face of God, and saying that I did not want anything. I was very sure that he would accomplish all his wise and good pleasure, and with that my soul was entirely satisfied.

Here I lost that great struggle in which I had been engaged for so long a time, and began to preach to the congregation in accordance with my new and enlarged experience. There was a considerable number in the church who understood me, and they saw from my preaching what had been, and what was, passing in my mind. I presume the people were more aware than I was myself of the great change in my manner of preaching. Of course my mind was too full of the subject to preach anything except a full and present salvation in the Lord Jesus Christ.

At this time it seemed as if my soul was wedded to Christ in a sense in which I had never had any thought or conception before. The language of the Song of Solomon was as natural to me as my breath. I thought I could understand well the state of mind he was in when he wrote that song, and concluded then, as I have thought ever since, that that song was written by him after he had been reclaimed from his great backsliding. I not only had all the freshness of my first love but a vast access to it continually. Indeed, the Lord lifted me so much above anything that I had experienced before and taught me so much of the meaning of the Bible, of Christ's relationship to me, and power, and willingness, that I often found myself saying to him, "I had not known or conceived that any such thing was true." I then realized what is meant by the saying that he "is able to do exceeding abundantly above all that we ask or think." He did at that time teach me indefinitely above all that I had ever asked or thought. I had had no conception of the length and breadth, and height and depth and efficiency of his grace.

It seemed then to me that the passage "My grace is sufficient for you" meant so much that it was strange I had never understood it before.

I found myself exclaiming, "Wonderful! Wonderful!" as these revelations were made to me. I could understand then what was meant by the prophet when he said, "His name shall be called Wonderful, Counsellor, The mighty God, the everlasting Father, The Prince of Peace." I spent nearly all the remaining part of the winter, until I was obliged to return home, in instructing the people in regard to the fullness there was in Christ. But I found that I preached over the heads of the majority of the people. Many of them did not understand me, but there was a goodly number who did. They were wonderfully blessed in their souls and made more progress in the divine life than in all their lives before.

26

I labored that winter mostly for a revival among Christians. The Lord prepared me to do so by the great work he wrought in my own soul. Although I had had much of the divine life working in me, yet, as I said, what I found in the Lord that winter so far exceeded all that I had before experienced that at times I could not realize that I had ever before been truly in communion with God.

To be sure I had been, often and for a long time. This I knew when I reflected upon it and remembered through what I had so often passed. It appeared to me that winter that probably when we get to heaven our views and joys and holy exercises will so far surpass anything that we have ever experienced in this life that we shall hardly be able to recognize the fact that we had any religion while in this world. I had in fact oftentimes experienced inexpressible joys, and very deep communion with God. But all this had fallen so into the shade under my enlarged experience that frequently I would tell the Lord that I had never before had any conception of the wonderful things revealed in his blessed Gospel and the wonderful grace there is in Christ Jesus. I knew when I reflected upon it that this language was comparative, but still all my former experiences, for the time, seemed to be sealed up and almost lost sight of.

As the great excitement of that season subsided, and my mind became more calm, I saw more clearly the different steps of my Christian experience, and came to recognize the connection of things as all wrought by God from beginning to end. But since then I have never had those great struggles and long protracted seasons of agonizing prayer that I had often experienced. It is quite another thing now to prevail with God, in my own experience, from what it was before. I can come to God with more calmness because I come with more perfect confidence. He enables me to rest in him and let everything sink into his perfect will with much more readiness than ever before the experience of that winter.

I have felt since then a religious freedom, a religious buoyancy and delight in God and in his Word, a steadiness of faith, a Christian liberty and overflowing love, that I had experienced only occasionally before. I do not mean that such exercises had been rare to me before, for they had been frequent and often repeated, but never abiding as they have been since. My bondage seemed to be at that time entirely broken, and since then I have had the freedom of a child with a loving parent. It seems to me that I can find God within me in such a sense that I can rest upon him and be quiet, lay my heart in his hand, and nestle down in his perfect will without any anxiety.

I speak of these exercises as habitual since that period, but I cannot affirm that they have been altogether unbroken, for in 1860, during a period of sickness, I had a season of great depression and wonderful humiliation. But the Lord brought me out of it into an established peace and rest.

A few years after this season of refreshing that beloved wife of whom I have spoken died. This was to me a great affliction. However, I did not feel any murmuring or the least resistance to the will of God. I gave her up to God without any resistance whatever that I can remember. But it was to me a great sorrow.

The night after she died I was lying in my room alone while some Christian friends were sitting in the parlor watching throughout the night. I had been asleep for a little while, and as I awoke the thought of my bereavement flashed over my mind with such power! My wife was gone! I would never hear her speak again nor see her face! Her children were motherless! What should I do? My brain seemed to reel as if my mind would swing from its pivot. I rose instantly from my bed exclaiming, "I shall be deranged if I cannot rest in God!" The Lord soon calmed my mind for that night, but still at times seasons of sorrow would come over me that were almost overwhelming.

One day I was upon my knees, communing with God upon the subject, and all at once he seemed to say to me, "You loved your wife?"

"Yes."

"Well, did you love her for her own sake or for your sake? Did you love her or yourself? If you loved her for her own sake, why do you sorrow that she is with me? Should not her happiness with me make you rejoice instead of mourn if you loved her for her own sake? Did you love her," he seemed to say to me, "for my sake? If you loved her for my sake, surely you would not grieve that she is with me. Why do you think of your loss, and lay so much stress upon that, instead of thinking of her gain? Can you be sorrowful when she is so joyful and happy? If you loved her for her own sake, would you not rejoice in her joy and be happy in her happiness?"

I can never describe the feelings that came over me when I seemed to be thus addressed. It produced an instantaneous change in the whole state of my mind. From that moment, sorrow, on account of my loss, was gone forever. I no longer thought of my wife as dead but as alive in the midst of the glories of heaven. My faith was, at this time, so strong and my mind so enlightened that it seemed as if I could enter into the very state of mind in which she was in heaven. And if there is any such thing as communing with an absent spirit, or with one who is in heaven, I seemed to commune with her. Not that I ever supposed she was present in such a sense that I communed personally with her. But it seemed as if I knew what her state of mind was there, what profound, unbroken rest in the perfect will of God. I could see that that was heaven, and I experienced it in my own soul. I have never, to this day, lost the blessing of these views. They frequently recur to me as the very state of mind in which the inhabitants of heaven are, and I can see why they are in such a state of blessedness.

My wife had died in a heavenly frame of mind. Her rest in God was so perfect that it seemed to me in leaving this world she only entered into a fuller apprehension of the love and faithfulness of God, so as to confirm and make perfect forever her trust in God and her union with his will. These are experiences in which I have lived a great deal since that time.

But in preaching, I have found that nowhere can I preach those truths on which my own soul delights to live, and be understood, except by a very small number. I have found only a very few, even of my own people, appreciate and receive those views of God and Christ and the fullness of his free salvation upon which my own soul still delights to feed. Everywhere I am obliged to come down to where the people are in order to make them understand me. And in every place where I have preached, for many years, I have found the churches in so low a state as to be utterly incapable of understanding and appreciating what I regard as the most precious truths of the whole Gospel.

When preaching to impenitent sinners, I am obliged,

of course, to go back to first principles. In my own experience I have so long passed these outposts and first principles that I cannot live upon those truths. I, however, have to preach them to the impenitent to secure their conversion. When I preach the Gospel, I can preach the atonement, conversion, and many of the prominent views of the Gospel that are appreciated and accepted by those who are young in the religious life, and by those also who have been long in the church of God and have made very little advancement in the knowledge of Christ. But it is only now and then that I find it really profitable to the people of God to pour out to them the fullness that my own soul sees in Christ. Everywhere the majority of professing Christians do not understandingly embrace those truths. They do not object, they do not oppose, and so far as they understand, they are convinced. But as a matter of experience, they are ignorant of the power of the highest and most precious truths of the Gospel of salvation in Christ Jesus.

27

Having had repeated and urgent invitations to visit England and labor for the promotion of revivals in that country, I embarked with my wife* in the autumn of 1849, and after a stormy passage, we arrived at Southampton early in November. I had hardly arrived in England before I began to receive multitudes of invitations to preach for the purpose of taking up collections for different objects: to pay the pastor's salary, to help pay for a chapel, or to raise money for the Sunday school, or for some such object. And had I complied with their requests I could have done nothing else. But I declined to go in answer to any such call. I told them I had not come to England to get money for myself or for them. My object was to win souls to Christ.

On our arrival in Southampton we were met by the pastor of the church in Houghton, a village situated midway between the market towns of Huntington and Saint Ives. When we had rested a few days, I began my labors in the village chapel. Our host threw his house open morning, noon and evening, and invited friends far and near to come and pay him a visit. They came in great numbers, so that his table was surrounded at nearly every meal with different persons

---

*Mr. Finney's second wife, Mrs. Elizabeth F. Atkinson of Rochester. Ed.

who had been invited in that I might have conversation with them, and that they might attend our meetings. My host was a Quaker, but he was entirely nonsectarian in his views and was laboring, in an independent way, directly for the salvation of the people around him. He had wealth, and his property was constantly and rapidly increasing. For religious purposes he would spend his money like a prince, and the more he spent the more he had to spend.

A revival began immediately and spread among the people. The work spread among those who came from the neighboring villages. They heard and gladly received the word. I soon accepted the invitations of ministers to labor in their several pulpits. The congregations were crowded everywhere, a great interest was excited, and after preaching the numbers that would gather into the rooms under an invitation for inquirers was large. Their largest rooms would be packed with inquirers whenever a call was made to go there for instruction.

For a while I labored with Rev. John Campbell in the old tabernacle of Whitefield in London. Dr. Campbell was a successor of Whitefield. His voice was such that he did not preach but gave his time to editing religious periodicals. He lived in the parsonage in which Whitefield resided and used the same library that Whitefield had used. Whitefield's portrait hung in the tabernacle study. The savor of his name was still there, yet I must say that the spirit that had been upon him was not very apparent in the church at the time I was there. Dr. Campbell still drew a salary, but he supplied his pulpit by employing, for a few weeks at a time, the most popular ministers to preach to his people. Such a constant change in the ministry did not cause religion to flourish in the church.

The tabernacle was large. It was compactly seated and could accommodate three thousand persons. After preaching for several weeks I knew it was time to call for inquirers. But Dr. Campbell, I could tell, had no such idea in his mind. The practice in that church was to hold a communion service every other Sunday evening. On these occasions they would have a short sermon, then dismiss the congregations. All would leave except those who remained to celebrate communion.

On this particular Sunday morning I said to Dr. Campbell, "You have a communion service tonight, and I must have a meeting of inquiry at the same time. Have you a room anywhere on the premises to which I can invite inquirers after preaching?"

He hesitated and expressed doubts whether there were any that would attend such a meeting. However, as I pressed the matter upon him he replied, "Yes, there is the infants' room, to which you might invite them."

I inquired how many persons it could accommodate. He replied, "From twenty to thirty, perhaps forty."

"Oh," I said, "that is not half large enough. Have you not a larger room?"

At this he expressed astonishment and inquired if I thought there was interest enough in the congregation to warrant any such invitation as I had intended to give. I told him there were hundreds of inquirers in the congregation.

But at this he laughed and said it was impossible.

I asked him if there was not a larger room.

"Why yes," he said, "there is the schoolroom. But that will hold fifteen or sixteen hundred. Of course you don't want that."

"Yes," said I, "that is the very room. Where is it?"

Said he, "Mr. Finney, remember you are in England, and in London, and that you are not acquainted with our people. You might get people to attend such a meeting in America, but you will not get people to attend here. Remember that our evening service is out before the sun is down at this time of year. And do you suppose that in the middle of London, under an invitation to those that are seeking the salvation of their souls, people will single themselves out right in the daytime to attend such a meeting as that?"

"Dr. Campbell, I know what the state of the people is better than you do. The Gospel is as well adapted to the English people as to the American people, and I have no fears at all that the pride of the people will prevent their responding to such a call any more than it would the people in America."

After a good deal of discussion, the doctor reluctantly consented. He gave me particular directions to the place, which was a short distance from the tabernacle.

We then went to the meeting and I preached in the morning and again at evening, that is, at six o'clock. I preached a short sermon and then informed the people of what I desired. I called upon all who were anxious for their souls and who would like to make their peace with God immediately to attend a meeting for instruction. I was very particular in regard to who were invited. I said, "Professing Christians are not invited to attend this meeting. There is to be a communion service here. Let them remain here. Careless sinners are not invited to this meeting. Those, and those only, are invited who are not Christians but who are anxious for the salvation of their souls and wish instruction upon the question of their present duty to God."

This I repeated so as not to be misunderstood. I was determined not to have the mass of people go into that room, but I felt entirely confident that there was a great amount of conviction in the congregation, and that there were hundreds prepared to respond to such a call. I then dismissed the meeting and the congregation retired.

Dr. Campbell nervously and anxiously looked out of the window to see which way the congregation went, and to his great astonishment the street was crowded with people pressing to get to the schoolroom. I went with the crowd and waited at the entrance until the multitude went in. When I entered, I found the room packed. I soon discovered that the congregation was pressed with conviction in such a manner that great care needed to be taken to prevent an explosion of irrepressible feeling. It was but a very short time before Dr. Campbell himself came in. Observing such a crowd gather, he was full of anxiety to be present, and consequently hastened through with his communion service and came into the meeting of inquiry. He looked amazed at the crowd present and especially at the amount of feeling evident.

I addressed them for a short time on the question of immediate duty, and endeavored to make them understand that God required of them then and there to yield themselves entirely to his will and to accept Jesus as their only Redeemer. I had been in England long enough to feel the necessity of being very particular in giving them such instructions as would do away with their idea of waiting God's time. London is, and long has been, cursed with hyper-calvinistic preaching. I tried therefore in my instructions to guard them on the one hand against hyper-calvinism, and on the other against that low Arminianism in which I supposed many of them had been educated.

After I had laid the gospel net thoroughly around them, I then prepared to draw it ashore. As I was about to ask them to kneel down and commit themselves entirely and forever to Christ, a man cried out in the greatest distress of mind that he had sinned away his day of grace. I saw that there was danger of an uproar and I hushed it down as best I could. I called on the people to kneel down but to keep so quiet that they could hear every word of the prayer that I was about to offer. By a valiant effort, they kept so still as to hear what was said, although there was a great sobbing and weeping in every part of the house.

I then dismissed the meeting. After this I held similar meetings with similar results, frequently on Sunday evenings, while I remained with that congregation, which was in all nine months. The interest extended so far that the inquirers could not be accommodated in the schoolroom. Frequently when I saw that the impression on the congregation was very general and deep, after giving them suitable instructions and bringing them face to face with the question of unqualified and present surrender of all to Christ, I would simply call on those who were prepared to do this to stand up in their places while we offered them to God in prayer. The aisles of the church were so narrow and packed that it was impossible to use what is called the anxious seat, or for people to move about in the congregation.

Frequently when I made these calls for people to rise to accept Christ while we offered them in prayer, many hundreds would rise. On some occasions, if the house seated as many as was supposed, not less than two thousand people sometimes rose when an appeal was made. Indeed, it would appear from the pulpit as if nearly the whole congregation rose. And yet I did not call upon church members but simply inquirers to stand.

When I left London there were four or five different Episcopal churches that were holding daily meetings and making efforts to promote a revival. In every instance they were greatly blessed and refreshed. It was ten years before I visited London again to labor, and I was told that the work had never ceased; that it had been going on and enlarging its borders, spreading in different directions.

I have said my mind was greatly exercised about the state of London. I was scarcely ever more drawn out in prayer for any city or place than I was for London. Sometimes when I prayed, in public especially with the multitudes before me, it seemed as if I could not stop praying, and that the spirit of prayer would almost draw me out of myself, in pleadings for the people and for the city at large.

After I had preached for Dr. Campbell about four months and a half, I became very hoarse. My wife's health also became much affected by the climate and by our intense labors. And here I must begin more particularly to tell of what God did by her.

Up to this time she had attended and taken part only in meetings for women, and those were such a new thing in England that she had done but little thus far. But while we were at Dr. Campbell's a request was made that she attend a tea meeting of poor women without education and without religion. Tea meetings, as they are called, are held in England to bring together people for any special object. Such a meeting was called by some of the benevolent Christian gentlemen and ladies, and my wife was urgently requested to attend it. She consented, having no thought that gentlemen would remain in the meeting while she spoke.

However, when she got there she found the place crowded, and in addition to the women a considerable number of men who were greatly interested in the results of the meeting. She waited a little, expecting that they would leave. But as they remained, expecting her to take charge of the meeting, she rose and apologized for being called to speak in public, informing them that she had never been in the habit of doing so. She had then been my wife but a little more than a year and had never been with me to labor in revivals until we went to England.

She made an address at this meeting, as she informed me after she came to our lodgings, of about three-quarters of an hour in length, and with very good results. The poor women present seemed to be greatly moved and interested, and when she had finished speaking, some of the men rose and expressed their great satisfaction at what they had heard. They said they had had prejudices against women speaking in public, but they could see no objection to it under such circumstances, for they saw that it was obviously calculated to do great good. They therefore requested her to speak at other similar meetings, which she did.

When she told me what she had done she said she did not know but that it would excite the prejudices of the people of England and perhaps do more harm than good. I feared this myself, and so expressed myself to her. Yet I did not advise her to keep still, but encouraged her to go ahead. From that time she became more and more accustomed to that kind of labor while we remained in England, and after we returned home she continued to labor with her own sex wherever we went.

Everyone acquainted with London is aware that from early in November until March the city is gloomy and has a miserable atmosphere either to breathe or speak in. We had arrived there early in May. In September my gracious Quaker host from Houghton called on us, and seeing the state of health we were in, he said, "This will never do. You must go to France, or somewhere on the continent where they cannot understand your language, for there is no rest for you in England as long as you are able to speak at all." He handed me fifty pounds sterling to meet our expenses.

We went to Paris and various other places in France, keeping ourselves as quiet as possible. The influence of the change of climate upon my wife's health was very marked. She recovered her full strength very rapidly. I gradually got over my hoarseness. After an absence of about six weeks we returned to our labors in the tabernacle, where we continued to labor until early the next April when we left for home. On the day that we sailed, a multitude of people who had been interested in our labors gathered upon the wharf. Thus closed our labors in England on our first visit there.

28

We arrived back at Oberlin in May, 1851, and after the usual labors of the summer we left in the autumn for New York City, expecting to spend the winter there. But after preaching a short time I found so many hindrances in the way of our work that I left and accepted an invitation to go to Hartford and hold a series of meetings.

In this Hartford revival there was a great deal of praying. The young converts especially gave themselves to much prayer. One evening one of the young converts after the evening services invited another to go home with him, and they would hold a time of prayer together. The Lord was with them, and the next evening they invited others, and the next evening more still until the meeting became so large that they were obliged to divide it. These meetings were held after the preaching service. The second meeting soon became too large, and that again was divided. These meetings multiplied until the young converts were almost universally in the habit of holding meetings for prayer in different places after the preaching service. They invited inquirers to these meetings and such as wished to be prayed for. This led to quite an organized effort among the converts for the salvation of souls.

A very interesting state of things developed at this time in the public schools. I was informed that ministers had agreed that they would not visit the public schools and make any religious efforts there because it excited jealousy on the part of different denominations. One morning when a large number of lads came together they were so affected that they could not study, and asked their teacher to pray for them. He was not a professing Christian and sent for one of the pastors, informing him of the state of things and requesting him to come and hold some religious service with them. He declined, saying that there was an understanding among the pastors that they would not go to the public schools to hold any religious services. The teacher sent for another, and still another, but they told him he must pray for the scholars himself. This brought a severe pressure upon him. It resulted in his giving his own heart to God, and in taking measures for the conversion of the students. There were a goodly number of the scholars in the various public schools who were converted at that time.

Mrs. Finney established prayer meetings for ladies, which were held in the churches. These meetings were attended by large numbers of women and became most effective. The ladies were entirely united, very much in earnest, and became a principal power, under God, in promoting his work there.

The next winter we left Oberlin at the usual season and started east to occupy a field of labor to which we had been invited. While we were in Hartford the previous winter, we had a very pressing invitation to go to the city of Syracuse to labor which we accepted. I preached there one Sunday and learned so much about the state of things that I remained another Sunday. Soon I began to perceive a movement among the dry bones. I could not see my way clear to leave, and I kept on from Sunday to Sunday. The Lord removed the obstacles and brought Christian people nearer together.

Here again Mrs. Finney established ladies' meetings
with great success. A great many interesting facts occurred in her meetings that winter. Christians of different denominations seemed to flow together, after
awhile, and all the difficulties that had existed between
them seemed to disappear. The Presbyterian and Congregational churches were all without pastors while
I was there, and so none of them opened their doors
to receive the converts. I was very willing that this
should be so, as I knew that there was great danger,
if they began to receive the converts, that jealousies
would spring up and mar the work.

There is one circumstance I have often heard Mrs.
Finney relate which occurred in her meetings. Her
ladies' meetings were composed primarily of the more
intelligent ladies in the different churches. But there
was an elderly and uneducated old woman who attended
their meetings who used to speak, apparently to the
annoyance of the ladies. Somehow she had the impression that it was her duty to speak at every meeting.
Sometimes she would get up and complain of the Lord,
that he laid it upon her to speak in the meeting, while
so many ladies of education were allowed to attend
and take no part. She wondered why it was that God
made it her duty to speak while these fine ladies, who
could speak so much better, were allowed to attend
and "have no cross," as she expressed it, "to take
up." She seemed always to speak in a whining and
complaining manner. The fact that she felt it her duty
to take part in every meeting annoyed and discouraged
my wife. She saw that it did not interest the ladies
and it seemed to her rather an element of disturbance.

But after things had gone on in this way for some
time, one day this same old woman rose in the meeting
and a new spirit was upon her. As soon as she opened
her mouth it was apparent to everybody that a great
change had come over her. She had come to the meeting

full of the Holy Spirit, and she poured out her fresh experience to the astonishment of all. The ladies were greatly interested in what the old woman said, and she related what the Lord had done for her with an earnestness that carried conviction to every mind. All turned and leaned toward her, to hear every word that she said. The tears began to flow, and a great movement of the Spirit seemed to be visible at once throughout the meeting. Such a remarkable change wrought immense good, and the old woman became a favorite. After that they expected to hear from her and were greatly delighted from meeting to meeting to hear her tell what the Lord had done, and was doing, for her soul.

I found in Syracuse a Christian woman whom they called "Mother Austin," a woman of most remarkable faith. She was poor and entirely dependent upon the charity of the people for subsistence. She was an uneducated woman and had been brought up in a family of very little opportunity. But she had such faith as to secure the confidence of all who knew her. The conviction seemed to be universal among both Christians and unbelievers that Mother Austin was a saint. I do not think I ever witnessed greater faith in its simplicity than was manifested by that woman. A great many facts were related to me respecting her that showed her trust in God, and in what a remarkable manner God provided for her wants from day to day. She said to me on one occasion, "Brother Finney, it is impossible for me to suffer for any of the necessaries of life because God has said to me, 'Trust in the Lord and do good; so will you dwell in the land, and surely you will be fed.'" She related to me many facts in her history, and many facts were related to me by others, illustrative of the power of her faith.

She told me that one Saturday evening a friend of hers, an impenitent man, called to see her. After conversing awhile he offered her a five dollar bill as he was leaving. She said she felt an inward admonition not to take it. She felt that it would be an act of self-righteousness on the part of that man, and might do him more harm that it would do her good. She therefore declined to take it. She had just enough wood and food in the house to last over the Lord's Day, and she had no means whatever of obtaining any more. But still she was not at all afraid to trust God in such circumstances, as she had done for so many years.

On Sunday there came a violent snowstorm. On Monday morning the snow was several feet deep, and the streets were blocked up so that there was no getting out without clearing the way. She had a young son who lived with her, the two composing the whole family. They arose in the morning and found themselves snowed in on every side. They had just enough fuel for a little fire, and soon the boy began to ask what they should have for breakfast. She said, "I do not know, my son, but the Lord will provide." They looked out and found that nobody could pass the streets.

The lad began to weep bitterly, concluding that they would freeze and starve to death. However, she went on and made such preparations as she could, to provide for breakfast, if any should come, and set her table. Very soon she heard a loud talking in the streets and went to the window to see what it was. She saw a man in a single sleigh and some men with him, shoveling the snow so that the horse could get through. Up they came to her door, and behold! they had brought her plenty of fuel and food, everything to make her comfortable for several days.

But time would fail to tell the many instances in which she was helped in a manner as striking as this. Indeed, it was known throughout the city that Mother Austin's faith was like a bank and that she never suffered for want of the necessities of life because she drew on God.

When we were about to leave Syracuse in the spring

I gave notice from the pulpit, on my own responsibility, that on the next Sunday we would hold a communion service to which all Christians who truly loved the Lord Jesus Christ were invited. That was one of the most interesting communion services I ever witnessed. The church was filled with communicants. Two very aged ministers attended and helped at the communion service. There was a great melting in the congregation, and a more loving and joyful communion of the people of God I never saw anywhere.

29

In the autumn of 1855 we were called again to the city of Rochester to labor for souls. When I had earlier stated my objections to going to labor in Rochester again, the brother who came after me set all that aside by saying, "The Lord is going to send you to Rochester, and you will go to Rochester this winter, and we shall have a great revival." When I arrived there I was soon convinced that it was of God.

Mrs. Finney was well acquainted in Rochester, having lived there for many years and having witnessed the two great revivals in which I had labored that preceded this one. She took an absorbing interest in this revival, and labored, as usual, with great zeal and success.

I never preached anywhere with more pleasure than in Rochester. I had labored in other cities where the people were even more highly educated than in Rochester. But in those other cities the views and habits of the people were more stereotyped—the people more fastidious and more afraid of changes than in Rochester. In New England I found a high degree of general education, but a timidity, a stiffness, a formality, and a stereotyped way of doing things that made it impossible for the Holy Spirit to work with as much freedom and power.

There was one of the judges living in Rochester

who seemed to be possessed of a chronic skepticism. He was a reader and a thinker, a man of great refinement and of great intellectual honesty. His wife, having been converted under my ministry, was a particular friend of mine. I had very thorough conversations with that man. He always freely confessed to me that my arguments were conclusive, and that his intellect was carried by the preaching and the conversation. He said to me, "Mr. Finney, always in your public discourses you carry me right along with you. But while I assent to the truth of all that you say, I do not feel right. Somehow my heart does not respond."

He was one of the loveliest of unconverted men, and it was both a grief and a pleasure to converse with him. His candor and intelligence made conversation with him on religious subjects a great pleasure, but his chronic unbelief made it exceedingly painful. So far as I know he has never been converted. His praying and idolized wife has gone to her grave. His only child, a son, was drowned before his eyes. After these calamities had befallen him I wrote him a letter, trying to win him to a source from which he could get consolation. He replied in all kindness, but dwelling upon his loss he said there could be no consolation that could meet a case like that. He was truly blind to all the consolation he could find in Christ. He has lived in Rochester through one great revival after another, but still so far as I know, he has mysteriously remained in unbelief.

Several of the lawyers who were converted at this time in Rochester gave up their profession and went into the ministry. Among these was a young lawyer who appeared to be soundly converted. For some reason with which I am not acquainted, he went to Europe and to Rome and finally became a Roman Catholic priest. He has been laboring zealously for years to promote revivals among them, holding protracted meetings. He told me himself, when I met him in England, that he was trying to accomplish in the Roman Catholic Church what I was endeavoring to accomplish in the Protestant church. He seems to be an earnest minister of Christ, given up, heart and soul, to the salvation of Roman Catholics. When I was in England he was there, sought me out, came very affectionately to see me, and we had just as pleasant an interview as if we had both been Protestants.

The next autumn we accepted an invitation to labor again in Boston. The first sermon I preached there was directed to the searching of the church, for I always began by trying to stir up a thorough and pervading interest among professing Christians, to secure the reclaiming of those that were backslidden and search out those that were self-deceived and if possible bring them to Christ.

After the congregation was dismissed and the pastor was standing with me in the pulpit, he said to me, "Brother Finney, I wish to have you understand that I need to have this preaching as much as any member of this church. I have been very much dissatisfied with my religious state for a long time, and have sent for you on my own account, and for the sake of my own soul, as well as for the sake of the souls of the people." He seemed thoroughly to give his heart to God. And one evening at a prayer and conference meeting he related to the people his experience and told them that he had been converted that day.

This of course produced a deep impression upon the church and congregation, and also upon the city quite extensively. Some of the pastors thought it was injudicious for him to make a thing of that kind so public. But I did not regard it in that light. It was the best means he could use for the salvation of his people.

The winter of 1857-58 will be remembered as the

time when a great revival prevailed throughout all the northern states. It swept over the land with such power that for a time it was estimated that not less than fifty thousand conversions occurred in a single week. Daily prayer meetings were established throughout the length and breadth of the northern states.

In one of our daily prayer meetings in Boston that winter a gentleman rose and said, "I am from Omaha, Nebraska. On my journey east I have found a continuous prayer meeting all the way. The distance," he said, "is about two thousand miles from Omaha to Boston, and here was a prayer meeting about two thousand miles in extent."

This revival is of so recent a date that I need not enlarge upon it, because it became almost universal throughout the northern states. A divine influence seemed to pervade the whole land. Slavery seemed to shut it out from the South. The people there were in such a state of irritation, of vexation, and of committal to their peculiar institution of slavery, which had come to be assailed on every side, that the Spirit of God seemed to be grieved away from them. There seemed to be no place found for him in the hearts of the southern people at that time. But elsewhere it was estimated that during this revival not less than five hundred thousand souls were converted in this country. The New York *Tribune* at that time published several extras, filled with accounts of the progress of the revival in different parts of the United States.

The church and ministry in this country had become so extensively engaged in promoting the revival, and such was the blessing of God attending the labors of laymen as well as of ministers, that I made up my mind to return and spend another season in England, and see if the same influence would not pervade that country.

30

We sailed for Liverpool in December, 1858. Immediately on our arrival, I received a great number of letters from different parts of England expressing great joy at our return and inviting us to come and labor in many different fields. While I was in London I was invited very urgently to visit Edinburgh, Scotland. I remained three months in Edinburgh, preaching in one of the largest places of worship there. We had a very interesting revival in that place and many souls were converted. I also labored in Aberdeen for a time, and then went on to Bolton, where we arrived on Christmas Eve, 1859.

In this place the work of the Lord began immediately. We were received as guests by Mr. B——. He belonged to the Methodist denomination, was a man of sterling piety, and very unsectarian in his views and feelings. The evening after we arrived he invited a few friends for religious conversation and prayer, among them a lady who had been for some time in an inquiring state of mind. After we had had a little conversation we decided to have a season of prayer. My wife knelt near this lady of whom I have spoken, and during prayer she observed that she was much affected.

As we rose from our knees, Mrs. Finney took her by the hand and then beckoned to me across the room to come and speak with her. The lady had been brought up a Quaker, but had married a man who was a Methodist. For a long time she had been uneasy about the state of her soul, but had never been brought face to face with the question of present, instantaneous submission.

I responded to the call of my wife, went across the room and spoke with her. I saw in a moment that her distress of mind was profound. I therefore asked her if she would see me for a little time in personal conversation. She readily complied. We crossed the hall into another room, and then I brought her face to face at once with the question of instant submission and acceptance of Christ. I asked her if she would then and there renounce herself and everything else and give her heart to Christ.

She replied, "I must do it sometime, and I may as well do it now." We knelt down immediately, and she did truly submit to God.

After she had submitted we returned to the parlor, and the scene between herself and her husband was very affecting. As soon as she came into the room he saw such a change in her face that they seemed spontaneously to clasp each other in their arms, and knelt down before the Lord.

We were scarcely seated before the son of Mr. B—— came into the parlor, announcing that one of the servants was deeply moved. In a very short time that one also gave evidence of submission to Christ. Then I learned that another was weeping in the kitchen, and went immediately to her, and after a little conversation and instruction, she too appeared to give her heart to God. Thus the work had begun. The report of what the Lord was doing soon spread abroad, and people came in daily, almost hourly, for conversation.

Our first meeting was in the chapel occupied by Mr. Davison, who had sent for me to come to Bolton.

He was an Independent. His chapel was filled the first night. The meeting was opened by a Methodist minister, who prayed with great fervency and with a liberty that plainly indicated to me that the Spirit of God was upon the congregation, and that we would have a powerful meeting. I was invited to follow him with some remarks. I did so, and occupied a little time in speaking upon the subject of prayer. I tried to impress upon them as a fact that prayer would be immediately answered if they took the stumbling blocks out of the way and offered the prayer of faith. The word seemed to thrill through the hearts of Christians. Indeed, I have seldom addressed congregations upon any subject that seemed to produce a more powerful and beneficial effect than the subject of prayer. I find it so everywhere. Praying people are immediately stirred up by it, to lay hold of God for a blessing. They were in this place. That was a powerful meeting.

The Methodists are very strong in Bolton, and always have been since the day of Wesley. It was one of Wesley's favorite fields of labor, and they have always had an able ministry and strong churches. Their influence was far in the ascendancy there over all other religious denominations. I found among them both ministers and laymen who were most excellent and earnest laborers for Christ. But the Congregationalists too entered into the work with great spirit and energy, and while I remained there, all sectarianism seemed to be buried. They gave the town a thorough canvassing, and the canvassers met once or twice a week to make their reports.

The work went on and spread in Bolton until one of the ministers who had been engaged in directing the movement of canvassing the town said publicly that they found that the revival had reached every family in the city, and that every family had been visited. If we had had any place of worship large enough, we would probably have had ten thousand persons in the congregations from evening to evening. All we could do was to fill the hall to capacity and then use other means as we could to reach the multitudes in other places of worship.

On the second of August, 1860, we went to Liverpool, and on the morning of the third we left by steamer for New York. We had had very little rest in England for a year and a half, and those who are used to sea voyages will not wonder that I did not rest much during our voyage home. Indeed, we arrived a good deal exhausted. I myself was hardly able to preach at all. However, the state of things at Oberlin was such, and the time of year such, that I could not afford to rest. There were many new students there, and strangers had been moving into the place so that there was a large number of impenitent persons residing there at that time. The brethren were of the opinion that an effort must be made immediately to revive religion in the churches and to secure the conversion of the unconverted students.

We held daily prayer meetings in the church, which were well attended, the church generally full. At these meetings I labored hard to secure the legitimate results of a prayer meeting judiciously managed. Besides preaching twice on Sunday and holding a meeting of inquiry every Sunday evening, I preached several evenings during the week. In addition to these labors I was obliged to use up my strength in conversing with inquirers, who were almost constantly visiting me when I was out of the meetings. These labors increased in intensity and pressure from week to week. The revival became very general throughout the place and seemed to make a clean sweep of the unconverted in the place. After continuing these labors for four months, until I had very little rest day or night, I came home one

Sunday afternoon from one of the most powerful and interesting meetings I had ever witnessed, and was taken with a severe chill. From that time I was confined to my bed between two to three months.

Since 1860, although continually pressed by churches, east and west, to come and labor as an evangelist, I have not dared to comply with their request. I have been able, by the blessing of God, to perform a good deal of labor here, but I have felt inadequate to the exposure and labor of attempting to secure revivals in other places.

Last winter, 1866 and 1867, the revival was more powerful among the inhabitants at Oberlin than it had been since 1860. However, as before, I broke down in the midst and was unable to attend any more meetings. The brethren, however, went forward with the work, and it continued with great interest until spring. Thus I have brought my revival narrative down to this time, the 13th of January, 1868.

Yesterday, Sunday, we had a very solemn day in the First Church. I preached all day upon resisting the Holy Spirit. At the close of the afternoon service I called first upon all professing Christians who were willing to commit themselves against all resistance offered to the teachings of the Holy Spirit, to rise up and unite with us in prayer under the solemnity of this promise. Nearly all the professing Christians rose up without hesitation. I then called upon those that were not converted to rise up and take the same stand. I had been endeavoring to show that they were stiff-necked and uncircumcised in heart and ears, and had always resisted the Holy Spirit. I asked those of them who were willing to pledge themselves to do this no more, and to accept the teachings of the Holy Spirit and give themselves to Christ, also to rise up, and we would make them subjects of prayer. So far as

I could see from the pulpit nearly every person in the house stood up under these calls. We then had a very solemn season of prayer and dismissed the meeting.

Epilogue

Mr. Finney continued as pastor of the church in Oberlin until 1872, and as lecturer in the seminary until July, 1875. He wrote extensively up until the time of his death.

His last day on earth was a quiet Sunday in which he attended church as usual with his wife. After retiring that night he suffered severe pains in the area of his heart and died early the next morning, August 16, 1875, just two weeks before his 83rd birthday.

His complete autobiography was published the following year by the trustees of Oberlin College. This current edition has been condensed from its original size of some 550 pages of small print, but retains all the most significant and representative incidents of his remarkable life and ministry.

—Helen Wessel

HELEN WESSEL, B.A., is the founder and president of *Bookmates International, Inc.* She is the wife of Walter W. Wessel, Professor of New Testament at Bethel College, St. Paul, Minn., and is the mother of six children.

She took her B.A. from Sioux Falls College, Sioux Falls, S. Dak. She also attended Biola College, Fresno State College and Reedley Junior College, and has done graduate work at the University of Minnesota.

Wessel is presently a consultant to the International Childbirth Education Association, and was president of that organization from 1964 until 1966.

Her previous published works include *The Joy of Natural Childbirth* and *The Voice of Joy.* She co-authored the latter together with Neil and Peggy Verwey. Mrs. Wessel also edited *Childbirth Without Fear* and several other books.